KETO SLOW COO
Cookbook

**COOK FOOD SLOWLY
BURN FAT FAST**

**ESSENTIAL AND TASTY LOW CARB
RECIPES TO KICKSTART YOUR NEW
HEALTHY EATING STYLE**

Lilian Nielsen

TABLE OF CONTENTS

CHAPTER 15.

CONDIMENTS, SAUCES & BROTHS

CHAPTER 16.

VEGETABLES

CHAPTER 17.

DESSERTS

CHAPTER 18.

SPECIAL SECTION 1: BREAD

CHAPTER 19.

SPECIAL SECTION 2: EXTRA YUMMY MEALS

CHAPTER 20.

CHAPTER 1.
THE KETOGENIC DIET

Ketosis is a natural metabolic state of the body. This is where the diet gets its name from. During Ketosis, your body will get its fuel from fat cells. Sounds amazing, right? If your body could burn up all that fat for energy and keep it off your waist? Well, I have some more good news to give to you. That is precisely what it can do.

The entire process of ketosis is started by a tiny molecule in our body called a ketone. They are the lesser-known fuel molecules. While glucose is our body's main molecule for a source of energy, ketones are the only other fuel molecules that can provide our entire body—including our brain—with the energy it needs to function in the same way that glucose does.

Wow, what a mouth full! Basically, our ketone molecules are produced from our fat when there are low amounts of glucose in our system. Our body then burns the fatty ketone molecules up to use for energy.

So, how are ketones made? Simple! The fatty molecules that our body has stored are transported to the liver. Here in the liver, our fat becomes ketone molecules. These ketone molecules enter our bloodstream once they leave the liver and are used by cells in the body for fuel. The exact way that glucose is used.

The reason why ketosis is such a phenomenon is due to the ketone molecule. Unlike most other molecules, the ketone molecule can actually pass into the brain. This is the most important part of the Keto diet! With glucose no longer supplying the body's fuel, your brain needs to get its fuel from somewhere else, and since the brain cannot break down fat for energy, this could be a problem. Luckily, ketones can pass through to the brain and provide it with all the energy it needs in order to help you function. Incredible!

There are two ways to enter the ketosis state, and I will expand on them later on in this guide. Entering the ketosis state can happen through either intermittent fasting or maintaining a ketogenic diet.

History

It might surprise you to know that the keto diet was in popular use as early as the 1920s and 1930s. At least, this is when it became really popular as an alternative treatment for those who suffered from epilepsy.

The keto diet was introduced as a therapy for those with epilepsy, as studies had shown that previous fasting methods had helped reduce the severity of the condition. As other anticonvulsant therapies (such as new medications) became available, the keto diet was almost all but forgotten about.

Unfortunately, when the medications were unable to help around 30 percent of those that suffered from epilepsy, the ketogenic diet was re-introduced. It is still used as a recommendation today for those with epilepsy—particularly children—as its effects have still proven to be helpful in reducing and managing the seizures caused by epilepsy.

There were many years where doctors were discovering more about the benefits of entering a ketosis state for epilepsy. In fact, the treatment for epilepsy with fasting or a low carb diet dates back to ancient Greek physician's times. However, it was not until 1921 that an endocrinologist named Rollin Woodyat found the three water-soluble compounds in the liver that are known today as ketones. Dr. Rollin Woodyat was able to note that the ketone molecules were being produced by the liver as a result of fasting.

The same year that Woodyat found where the ketone molecules were being made, the diet received its official name from Russel Wilder and the Mayo Clinic before it was commonly used as an epileptic treatment. Shortly after anticonvulsant drugs became popular, doctors no longer received training in the keto diet. This caused a few doctors that tried to use it to implement it incorrectly. For optimal results with the keto diet, it is crucial to use it appropriately and follow it as needed to trigger the production and release of ketone molecules.

While the ketogenic diet took off in popularity as a therapy for those who suffered from epilepsy, it did not pass by unnoticed the effect it had on weight loss. Even though the keto diet almost disappeared due to a lack of use, around the 1990s, it made a reappearance. It began to grow more in notoriety for weight loss in the early 2000s.

After the 2000s, the keto diet took off in popularity and since then has been successfully used by thousands for weight loss. In recent years the keto diet has taken off due to its advantages in the health field as well; not only are the benefits of the keto diet linked to sustained weight loss and epilepsy, but other medical issues are reported to improve with the use of this diet.

About Ketosis

When we eat any type of food, our body processing these foods and various types of nutrients into different forms of energy such as proteins, carbohydrates, and fats; these are converted into the form of fuel using different metabolic processes. When your body absorbs the excess amount of protein and a high amount of carbohydrates, your body breaks it down into the form of glucose. The glucose provides cells with the quickest source of adenosine and three phosphates (ATP), which is the primary source of energy used by the human body. When your body consumes calories from proteins, fats, and carbohydrates, these calories increase the adenosine and three phosphates (ATP) levels in your body.

Your body stores this energy in two ways:

1. Glycogenesis: When the glucose level increases in your body, excess glucose are converted into the form of glycogen, and these glycogens are stored in the muscles and liver. Depending on your health, if you do not consume other calories within 7 to 24 hours' gap, your body automatically used these glycogens as an alternate energy source
2. Lipogenesis: when there is enough number of glycogens present in your liver and muscles, the extra glucose in your body is converted into the form of fats, and these facts are stored in your body; this process of storing fats is called lipogenesis. Glycogens are store in our body into a limited form, but fats have no limits for storage. These facts are sustaining our body for months without sufficient food.

In the unexpected situations when glucose and glycogens are insufficient to provide energy in your body, the fats are still used as a fuel in this process the alternate fuel source is producing called ketones.

When our body does not access any type of foods, or you are fasting, sleeping, or you have followed a ketogenic diet plan, at this stage, your body will break down some fats into energy molecules. These energy molecules are called ketones. Our brain uses sugar as a primary source of fuel so that the brain is much more dependent on the secondary energy source from ketones.

Benefits of Ketogenic Diet

Keto diet has lots of health benefits. Here are a few:

Easy to follow: This diet is easy to follow. This is mainly because you don't need to visit a dietician or a gym all the time. You can easily set up a schedule and follow it.
Available health benefits: This diet is rich in healthy dietary fats. These are required by your body for a number of health benefits.

No hungry: Since the diet is high in fat, you won't feel hungry very often. This is quite useful for those people who want to lose weight without changing their lifestyle.

Weight loss: The keto diet is known to reduce weight, on average, two pounds per week. This happens because of the fat that gets burned every day in the body.

Diabetics: This diet is excellent for diabetic patients. They are able to reduce their reliance on insulin. This happens because of the reduction in the supply of sugar in the body.

Less hunger: This diet makes you feel satiated throughout the day. This is good for individuals who have the issue of eating food under stress.

Lower blood pressure: This is also helpful for individuals who are struggling with high blood pressure. The diet, in the end, is capable of reducing the level of blood pressure.

Calmer mood: This diet is capable of improving the mood of people. This is another health advantage that comes with the diet.

Alzheimer's disease: This is also beneficial for people suffering from Alzheimer's disease. This is because the Ketogenic diet is known to decrease the beta-amyloid plaques in the brain.

Food to Eat

1. Eating unprocessed meat that is low in carbs is keto-friendly. Any organic or grass-fed meat is usually appropriate for a keto meal. Remember not to overeat on meat as your protein intake has to be moderate, and fat intake increased. If you eat too much meat, you overeat protein, and this gets converted to glucose for energy.
2. Fish and seafood are extremely keto-friendly. Try to get fresh and wild fish and avoid eating fish that were bred. Fatty fish, like salmon, is a great choice.
3. Eggs cooked in any form are keto-friendly. Try to acquire organic eggs.
4. Eat vegetables that grow above ground and avoid root vegetables like potatoes. Leafy and green vegetables are the best choice. You can also add cauliflower, zucchini, broccoli cabbage, and avocado to your diet. Cook them in fatty butter or oil to make them keto-friendly. Add more vegetables to your plate to make up for the grains you will avoid on keto.
5. High-fat dairy like butter, cheese, heavy cream, ketchup is suitable for a keto diet. The fatter, the better; however, try to avoid milk since milk sugar adds up. Always eat full-fat yogurt and keep away from the low-fat kind.
6. Nuts are great, but they should be eaten in moderation, as it is easy to overeat on them while snacking. Cashews should be eaten minimally since they contain a lot of carbs.
7. Low-sugar fruits like berries are keto-friendly in moderate amounts. Berries are a good substitute for sugary desserts. Add some full-fat whipping cream to a bowl of berries for your sweet fix.
8. Coffee is fine if you don't add any sugar. If you really need to add milk, ensure to use very little full-fat cream milk.
9. Water is the best liquid to hydrate with. You can add natural flavoring to your water, like cucumbers, lemons, to drink more often.

Food to Avoid

1. Grains in the form of wheat, barley, rye, sorghum, corn, bulgur, oats, quinoa, amaranth, rice, millet, buckwheat, etc. Avoid any bread, pasta, cookies, or even pizza crusts made from these grains. All grains should be avoided on a low carb diet since they will slow down the weight loss process.
2. Beans or legumes in the form of kidney beans, pinto beans, green peas, lima beans, fava beans, black beans, chickpeas, lentils, white beans, cannellini beans, etc. The high starch content in beans makes them unsuitable for a keto diet.
3. Fruits like bananas, oranges, pineapples, papaya, grapes, mangoes, apples, and tangerines. Avoid any fruit syrups, packaged fruit juices, fruit concentrates, or even dried fruits.

Everyone says fruits are healthy, but they are not keto-friendly due to their high sugar and carb content.

4. Starchy vegetables like sweet potatoes, peas, yams, corn, yucca, cherry tomatoes, carrots, or parsnips. These vegetables are not suitable for a keto diet as they contain high carbs.
5. Sugar in the form of honey, agave nectar, cane sugar, turbinado sugar, maple syrup, high fructose corn syrup, etc., should be avoided in any form.
6. Milk and low-fat dairy products like shredded cheese, fat-free butter, low-fat cream cheese, skimmed milk, low fat whipped cream, low-fat yogurt, etc.
7. Factory farmed animal products like grain-fed meats, canned meat, beef jerky, packaged sausages, bacon, chicken nuggets, fish sticks, corned beef, salami, hot dogs, or factory-farmed fish.
8. Unhealthy fats in the form of canola oil, safflower oil, soybean oil, grapeseed oil, sunflower oil, corn oil, or peanut oil.

CHAPTER 2.
THE SLOW COOKER

When it comes to dieting, some cooking methods are more suitable than others, e.g., grilling against frying. However, since Keto cooking is mostly about fats and then protein, you ideally want to try a convenient method that lets you preserve the nutritional goodness of your meals and, of course, the necessary fats. And this where slow cooking can come to the rescue. In particular, slow cooking has the following advantages when being on Keto, and you better try this out:

- It helps you control what goes inside and specifically the number of sugars and carbs. Since you will choose the ingredients to add, there will be no more guessing or having to read food labels to add low or zero sugar and carb ingredients like the ones listed earlier. This is perhaps the main advantage of using a slow cooker when on Keto. We have made this easier for you in this e-book by outlining the basic nutritional info for each recipe so you know exactly what goes inside.
- It maintains all the fats inside. By now, you have already realized that fats should be your main priority when on Keto. The issue with other cooking methods is that they dissolve and sometimes burn and evaporate the fat, e.g., grilling, which gets rids of the extra fat we need for keto and also makes the fat oxidize, which isn't healthy at all. On the contrary, slow cooking is one of the very few cooking methods that help preserve the original fat of the ingredients without oxidation, provided that you don't overcook your meals.
- It lets you prepare low carb yet fully nutritious liquids and sauces. A Slow Cooker can be used to make excellent chicken, beef, fish, and veggie stock, which are nutrient-dense yet contain little to none carbs—and yes, this is what we are looking for when on keto. You can later use any of these stocks as your base to cook healthy and delicious keto meats or veggie meals without adding carb-heavy sauces on top to add flavor. Since Slow Cookers work better with a bit of liquid, this kind of stocks and sauces can become your staples.

The Basics

Provided you use your slow cooker properly—and we'll attempt to outline all the basic steps as well as some tips and tricks, there is no reason why you shouldn't use your slow cooker when being on keto.

How to Use a Slow Cooker

If you are new to slow cooking, you don't have to worry about any fancy cooking techniques as the slow cooker will work its magic on your own, and the steps of setting up are so easy, even a small kid can cook with it.

When you buy a slow cooker, most manufacturers feature a low or high setting to choose for cooking your food, besides the on/off button. This may vary a bit from brand to brand, but usually, this is the main setting of a slow cooker. Read the manufacturer's instructions first to make sure you use it properly.

In general, the low setting is applicable to foods and ingredients that don't need much time to be cooked properly in the oven. In most cases, the low setting should be between ½ to 3 hours max. These are:

- Fish and seafood
- Sausages
- Boneless and skinless or tender cuts of meat, e.g., tenderloin
- Thinly cut veggies
- Soup Mixes

On the other hand, high setting, which takes 3-8 hours in most cases, is suitable for chunkier and tougher veggie or meat pieces like:

- Beef cuts, e.g., steaks, cubes, briskets, prime rib, oxtails
- Pork Chops
- Whole pork shoulders or pork bellies
- Spare ribs
- Celery Stalks
- Carrots (sliced thickly)

As a rule of thumb, the tougher the cut is, the slower cook time it will need to get juicier and tender--the softer or smaller it is, the less cook time it will need after setting this on.

- For convenience reasons and if you are in a hurry, you can add all the ingredients that a recipe calls chopped (if using meats or veggies) or peeled and wholesome without any other preparation. However, there are some tips that will help you with the best results when it comes to flavor, texture, and cook time. Here are some:
- Brown your meats and/or veggie chunks first. This is optional, but this is actually what helps retain the flavor of meats and veggies and makes them taste more roasty instead of boiled. It may sound time-consuming, but it's not--it only takes a couple of minutes on high heat and a bit of oil to get them to change color.
- Use softer ingredients last or in large, thicker pieces. This will ensure that they don't become too mushy or fall apart after slow-cooking. Some green leafy veggies like spinach, which wilt easily, could also be added last (during the last 30 minutes to an hour).
- Fill ideally ⊡ of your slow cooker, so there is a little extra space for the food to cook freely.

Filling it too much with solid and liquid ingredients will make the food steamed instead of simmered.

- Layer things properly. Some recipes are all about layering. In general, veggies (especially root vegetables) should come first, followed by meats and then liquids or spices.
- Don't raise the lid. You may be tempted to take a sneak peek or check if the food has been cooked properly, but if you do this more than once, you will end up losing valuable heat. Some recipes may require occasional stirring, but for most of the recipes, lifting the lid is unnecessary and a mistake.
- Use dairy in moderation. Some dairy products are fine when used in a slow cooker, while others will disintegrate and become a mess, so you better pay attention to the dairy products you add. Hard and fine cheeses like mozzarella and cheddar are fine when added last, but heavy creams and yogurts should be avoided altogether as they will break and fall apart.
- Use alcohol in moderation. While on a regular stovetop, alcohol will evaporate and add its aromas to the food without suffocating it; in a slow cooker using too much alcohol can make food taste just like that—pure, raw alcohol and cover the flavors and aromas of the rest of the dish. A little red or white wine is fine, but anything more than that should be avoided.
- Don't use poultry (chicken or duck) with the skin on unless you want to end up with a chewy, rubber-like skin that is also flavorless. If you want to add the skin, you can brown it first on a frying pan to make it crispier and flavorful.
- Don't overcook. Pay close attention to the recipe cook times and don't overcook something in hopes that it will get more tender and juicy—it will simply fall apart and become a mushy mess, especially if you are using fish or thinly cut veggies.
- Add the herbs last. Since herbs have a delicate flavor and aroma, putting them in the slow cooker too soon will dilute their scent to the point where you almost don't recognize it. Herbs, just like dairy, are best placed during the last 30 minutes of cooking.
- Last but not least, make sure you use some type of stock or any other liquid to submerge lean meat cuts, or your meat will dry up.

The Goals/Benefits of Using Slow Cooker

Slow cooking is a cooking method invented in the 1970s and is still widely popular today for quite a few reasons. In general, slow cookers have the following benefits for you:

- Less cooking preparation. Since the slow cooker works mostly on its own, you don't have to spare a great deal of time to prepare the ingredients or stir them up or even sit and watch as the slow cooker will cook everything automatically in the hours you've set this. All you need to do is turn it on, dump in the ingredients, and set it to your desired setting while you are free to do other things, for example, doing house chores or babysitting the kids. This is, of course, handy for busy people who don't have the time and energy to prepare nice meals—and if your slow cooker automatically turns off after the time you have set it to cook, there will be no worries that your food will burn or fall apart.

- More succulent and juicier results. Slow cooking, as its name suggests, slow cooks the food for hours, and that helps it retain all its juices—dried up and chewy food will be a thing of the past when you are using a slow cooker. Slow cooker especially works its magic in tough cuts of meats that tend to get chewy when using other cooking methods like frying or baking, for example, pork chops, beef chuck, pork bellies, and bone-in chicken or poultry.
- More flavorsome results. The slow cooking process, apart from maintaining the juices and the soft texture of your meals, will also help preserve their flavor. And the best part is, you won't need a bunch of ingredients to prepare something delicious. The slow cooking process slowly releases and blends all the flavors and aromas you place inside, and everything literally melts together.
- A slow cooker can help save valuable energy. This may not be so obvious to some, but slow cookers have been found to consume less electricity than conventional ovens who "eat" more energy resources to function. This, of course, will help you save money on electricity bills in the long run, especially if you use your slow cooker in place of your regular oven at least once a week.
- Slow Cooker is generally safe. The issue with other cooking methods is that they can be dangerous when you don't pay attention, like frying and grilling, and kids should avoid using these without any supervision. A slow cooker, on the contrary, can be used by almost everyone, even kids, as it releases slow and gradual amounts of heat, and there are no spills or excessive heat that might cause burns (well, unless you touch it inside when it's on).
- It's easy to clean up—no need to wash it underwater and soap like the rest of your utensils. A simple cloth, liquid, water, and vinegar, or even baking soda are enough to wipe out any remaining fats and dirt.

CHAPTER 3.
HOW IT CAN WORK FOR TYPE 2 DIABETICS

The Keto diet is very popular and is used widely to control Blood Sugar Levels. The diet is very restrictive on carbohydrates and focuses on the consumption of fats and proteins. The ketogenic diet has been shown to be very efficient in controlling blood sugar levels. It has been proven that the diet helps reduce the blood sugar level in patients with diabetes and is an effective way to reduce weight.

The keto diet is very simple and basically includes the consumption of no more than 25g of net carbs each day. The consumption of carbs in the form of protein and fats should be adequate for energy production. The protein ratio should be 1g for every Kg of body weight. Therefore, a person weighing 60kg should consume 60g of protein per day. The fat consumption should be double the protein and should be 20% of the total calorie consumption.

This diet has been recommended for patients with diabetes and has shown to be a powerful diet. This is because the diet helps in the insulin sensitivity of the body and hence helps in the reduction of blood sugar levels. The diet also helps in weight reduction and is effective in reducing excess weight. The keto diet helps in interfering with insulin receptors in the body and hence helps in the maintenance of glucose levels. The diet has a positive effect on increasing the body's use of ketones for energy instead of blood glucose. This is known as ketosis, which is the result of following a low carb diet.

The keto diet has many benefits compared to other diets. It helps in preventing Type 2 Diabetes, high cholesterol, and blood pressure. The diet also helps in lowering the chances of cardiovascular disease. This diet has also been linked to the prevention of Alzheimer's and cancer.

Ketone bodies are effective in losing weight. The ketogenic diet helps in losing excess weight by suppressing appetite, increasing fat oxidation and energy. Ketosis is the state of using ketone bodies to produce energy. Ketones present in the body are used to produce energy in the form of ATP, which is the main energy carrier in the body.

The ketogenic diet helps in losing weight by increasing the metabolism and the rate of fat oxidation. Ketosis helps in the breakdown of fat for energy and thereby prevents the accumulation of excess fat due to the consumption of excess calories. A ketogenic diet changes food preference and taste and suppresses appetite as it helps in the rapid energy increase.

Ketogenic Diet and Type 2 Diabetes

The ketogenic diet helps in the reduction of blood sugar levels and reduces the chances of developing diabetes. In patients with Type II Diabetes, the ketones effectively lower blood sugar. The diet is helpful in increasing the level of insulin sensitivity in the body. Although the increase in insulin sensitivity causes a reduction in the insulin requirement by the body, the diet has a positive effect on reducing blood sugar levels. The keto diet also helps in blocking the manufacturing of glucose by the liver in order to lower the blood sugar levels.

The keto diet helps in the prevention of insulin resistance and has a positive effect on Type II Diabetes by reducing the demand for insulin. The diet is an effective means of reducing the dependence on drugs utilized to control blood sugar levels. The diet also has a positive effect on the utilization of glucose by the body and helps in the prevention of hypoglycemia. It is also known to help in the slowing down of neuropathy, which is associated with diabetes.

Ketosis is the state of using ketone bodies to produce energy and helps in weight loss. The insulin is stimulated only when there is an insufficient amount of glucose in the blood and hence reduces the wasting of glucose in the body tissues.

From the above discussion, it is clear that the keto diet is very useful in treating diabetes. It helps in reducing the risk of hypoglycemia, which is associated with diabetes. It also helps in the prevention of diseases that are caused by diabetes, including heart disease and cancer.

The diet is also effective in weight loss by maintaining insulin sensitivity and has a positive effect on the production of ketone bodies. It is a successful way to lose weight and is useful in reducing the occurrence of Type 2 Diabetes in the long run.

The ketogenic diet is a diet that is quite effective in controlling blood sugar levels and is quite useful in regulating insulin in the body.

To conclude, the keto diet is really an excellent diet to follow and can help you lose weight. It is also recommended for type 2 diabetes and persons who are obese.

A recent study has shown that the keto diet for diabetes caused weight loss to be more rapid. To understand the findings of this study, you can read the study below.

In the recent study, the researchers involved in it found that the keto diet had a significant effect on diabetes and helped the patients in managing the disease. This was shown by the fact that the patients lost weight while on the keto diet and had an average weight loss of 37kg.

Before the study was conducted, there had been concerns regarding the position of the recipients of the diet regarding the possibility of having a negative effect on diabetes. Since the diet has been linked to accelerating the development of diabetes, the researchers wanted to understand the body's response to it.

The study was conducted on 90 people with Type 2 diabetes. These were all young people, and the average age of all the patients was 22 years. This made it clear that the diet was more suitable for young people than the elderly.

The researchers were interested in finding out if the keto diet could have any effect on people who did not know that they were diabetic. At the start of the study, they asked each patient about their experience of the diet before they had received the diet. The patients were asked if they knew that they had diabetes. The patients were also asked to fill out a questionnaire regarding their eating habits. Based on the patient's response to the questionnaire, they were divided into two groups; group 1 was diabetic patients who knew that they had diabetes, and group 2 contained those who did not know that they had diabetes.
Each group received physiotherapy.

The Results:

Group 1 had an average weight loss of 3.35kg. Group 2 had an average weight loss of 3.35kg. However, the patients who did not know that they had diabetes showed a slightly greater loss in weight than the patients who did. Not only did they lose the weight, but they also achieved a lower level of blood sugar (the reason they were on the diet).
The researchers thought that the reason for the greater weight loss was that the patients who did not know they had diabetes had a greater tendency to eat a lot of the foods that were probably not included in the diet. Since the diet is mainly composed of fats, this would suggest that the patients struggled to maintain the diet.
The results of the study are super and suggest that keto diets are wonderful for people with diabetes. This study showed that the keto diet had an effect on losing weight and managing diabetes. Initially, there was a doubt that the diet was not suitable for those who did not have diabetes; however, the study produced very positive results.

CHAPTER 4.
FREQUENTLY ASKED QUESTIONS

1.
Q: How does the Keto diet plan NOT contain carbs?
A: Carbs play a role in many crucial processes in our body. As a primary source of fuel, carbs have the potential to kick us out of ketosis. The Keto diet reduces total carbs intake to less than 50g a day (generally between 20 and 40g). The magic of Keto is in the removal of glucose. By removing glucose from your diet, your body is forced to seek an alternative fuel source – fat. This transition process will produce some uncomfortable symptoms. These are referred to as the Keto Flu.

2.
Q: Is Keto available for vegetarians and vegans?
A: Perfect Keto is available for both vegetarians and vegans. The Keto diet is a low carb diet plan that does not contain any animal products. On the other hand, a vegetarian diet is based on consuming vegetables, fruits, grains, nuts, beans, seeds, and legumes. Perfect Keto has found a way to incorporate meat replacers for cooked eggs, mayonnaise, and cream cheese.

3.
Q: How are carbohydrates processed?
A: Carbs are classified as mono and disaccharides. An example of a carbohydrate is glucose. It is the primary source of energy and can be found in grains, legumes, cereals, vegetables, and fruits. Glucose is constructed from carbon, oxygen, and hydrogen.

4.
Q: How does the Keto diet work?
A: First, you will need to determine your weight loss goal. Are you trying to lose 1kg or 75kg? It is a good idea to start slow. Have realistic expectations. Have strategies in place to avoid

plateaus and enjoy your efforts. You will need to consume 70 - 80% fat, 15 - 20% protein, and 5 - 10% carbohydrate.

5.
Q: When ketosis is reached, how will your body function on glucose?
A: Glucose is not required for any essential functions. They may be stored in the body for future use, but they are not needed in the body to function. The body will reach ketosis in 5 days, and it stays until the body finds a new fuel source.

6.
Q: How many calories does one need on this diet?
A: Since you are not consuming many carbs, your body will not be flooding your system with glucose. Therefore, there will be no insulin made in the body. Ketosis is the metabolic state for burning fat instead of glucose as fuel.

7.
Q: How is the Keto diet different from other diets?
A: The Keto diet is based on low-carb intake. For every gram of carbohydrate that you take in, your body turns it into glucose. When this happens, insulin is released in the body, therefore, making you store fat. This is where things are different on the Keto diet. You are going to avoid consuming sugars and carbs. When your body is so deprived of glucose, it will turn to fat stores as a source of energy.

8.
Q: What foods can you eat?
A: You will be allowed to eat foods like meat, fish, poultry, nuts, nut butter, seeds, eggs, cheese, berries, coconut products, and vegetables. Many of these foods are high in fat.

9.
Q: How can you incorporate carbs into your diet plan?
A: You will need to carefully count your carbohydrates. There is a different strategy for different things. You can add your favorite vegetables, green leafy vegetables, or even drink your vegetables as smoothies. However, if you add too much, you will be kicked out of ketosis. Once ketosis is reached, you may be able to reintroduce a small quantity of carbs.

10.
Q: What is the best way to lose weight on a low carb diet?
A: You do not need to exercise while on the Keto diet because the Keto diet has so many fat-burning properties.

CHAPTER 5.
TIPS

Knowing how to use a slow cooker best can be a game-changer in terms of simplifying your life. Here are a few tips that can make using your slow cooker an even more satisfying experience.

1. Meal plan and pre-prep your food as much as possible. Indeed, sometimes you can just throw random ingredients into a slow cooker and turn out a masterpiece. It is also true that sometimes that philosophy can result in a culinary disaster. I know that you are probably busy, and meal planning may or may not be on your priority list. However, you should try to give a little thought to what you might like to cook during the week. Taking a short time at the beginning of the week can save you significant time over the week if you prepare a particular dish or use specific ingredients, pre-wash, or cut them in advance to save yourself later. This is especially helpful if you are assembling a slow cooker full of goodness in the morning before you rush out the door.

2. To make your slow cooker meal a no-fuss event, prepare everything the night before. You can brown meat, cut vegetables, and assemble everything in the evening. Once it is built, place it in the refrigerator, grab it and get it going in the morning.

3. In most cases, slow cooker times can be adjusted to suit your schedule. The recipes in this book were created using a certain quantity of food at a low temperature to allow the dishes to take eight to ten hours to cook to perfection. If you would like to shorten that cook time, simply cut back a little on the ingredients and increase the temperature to high. Generally speaking, improving the condition can take two to four hours off the cooking time, depending on the dish.

4. Consider browning the meat. Many of the recipes in this book call for browning the meat or quickly sautéing some vegetables. Do you need to do this step? For that question, the answer is no. However, if you are looking for the highest quality results, then the answer is yes. Browning the meat before you place it in the slow cooker helps maintain the meat's moisture, flavor, and juiciness. When you sauté vegetables, you change the ingredient's

character and slightly taste something a little more desirable. Take onions, for instance. You can just place them in the slow cooker, and they will absorb juices and soften during cooking. The result is often delicious. Other times, you might want to sauté them a little to bring out their natural sweetness to a level that slow cooking alone cannot do.

5. When you brown your meat, don't forget to scrape the pan. There is a lot of goodness left in the bottom of a pan used to brown a meat piece. The same is true for the oils or moisture left after sautéing vegetables. Take the extra minute and scrape the pan into the slow cooker to keep all the different flavors.

6. Beware the dairy. If you follow a ketogenic diet, you are likely also enjoying creamy, full-fat dairy products daily. Full-fat dairy is excellent as it provides valuable nutrition and necessary fat calories. You can include full-fat dairy in your slow cooker creations. You have to be a little thought about how you do it. First of all, dairy that sits in the heat all day is going to curdle a bit. It is okay if it is small and mixed with other ingredients to help offset the effect. Sometimes the thickening that happens is just what you are expecting. However, in most cases, when you use more massive amounts of dairy, you will want to add it towards the end of the cooking time, usually in the last hour of cooking. This method will help maintain the texture and integrity of the dairy ingredients. It adds a little bit of time in the end, but it is well worth it.

7. Use the highest quality ingredients you can afford. When someone has a negative slow cooker experience, they used inferior ingredients and didn't mean you have to break the bank on all grass-fed or organic ingredients. That means to pay attention to where your money is best spent on quality and where you can afford to skimp. Also, cook with ingredients that are in season in your area whenever possible. A tomato that comes from the farmer across town will be far superior to one that traveled a thousand miles just to reach your grocer's shelf.

8. Don't overfill your slow cooker. For best results, your slow cooker should not be more than three-quarters of the way full. It allows plenty of room for the heat to circulate and cook everything evenly. If you find that your slow cooker is overstuffed, simply cut back on the bulky ingredients a little.

9. Resist the temptation to be lifting the lid and inhaling the savory aroma constantly. Yes, it smells great. However, you are disrupting the cooking process by allowing the heat to escape. Then the slow cooker has to work to get back up to the proper cooking temperature again.

10. Consider the placement of the ingredients in your slow cooker. One of the best features of a slow cooker is the "dump and go" potential. Slow cooker meals are generally low fussing and require little more than tossing the ingredients in and turning it on. There are times, though, when a little forethought about how the elements are placed can make a big difference to the result. The most heat is going to come from the bottom of the device. This means that what you put on the bottom is going to have more surface-to-surface heat. Sometimes, you might want this to be the meat.

11. Cut your ingredients in uniform pieces and keep texture in mind. Raw pumpkin is quite dense and can be cut into smaller, even pieces to ensure they are cooked to tender perfection. Mushrooms, on the other hand, cook relatively quickly and should be added in large chunks, or even in the last hour or two of cooking, if you will be home to add them.

Spinach and other greens should be added a short while before serving. When this is possible, give them time to wilt.

12. The meat thermometer is your friend. Even if that roast has been in there for eight hours and it looks delectably done, take a minute and stick a meat thermometer in it. For most meats that are not beef, you want a temperature of 160°F. With meat, you can have a bit more of a range depending upon the doneness you prefer. As a reference, 140°F was considered medium-rare for beef.

13. Your slow cooker not only makes leftovers super easy, but they often taste even better. The slow cooking process gives the ingredients more time together to build up the flavor. If you have bits, refrigerate them overnight and turn the slow cooker back on the next day. Add a little extra liquid if you need to for moisture.

CHAPTER 6.
BREAKFAST & BRUNCH

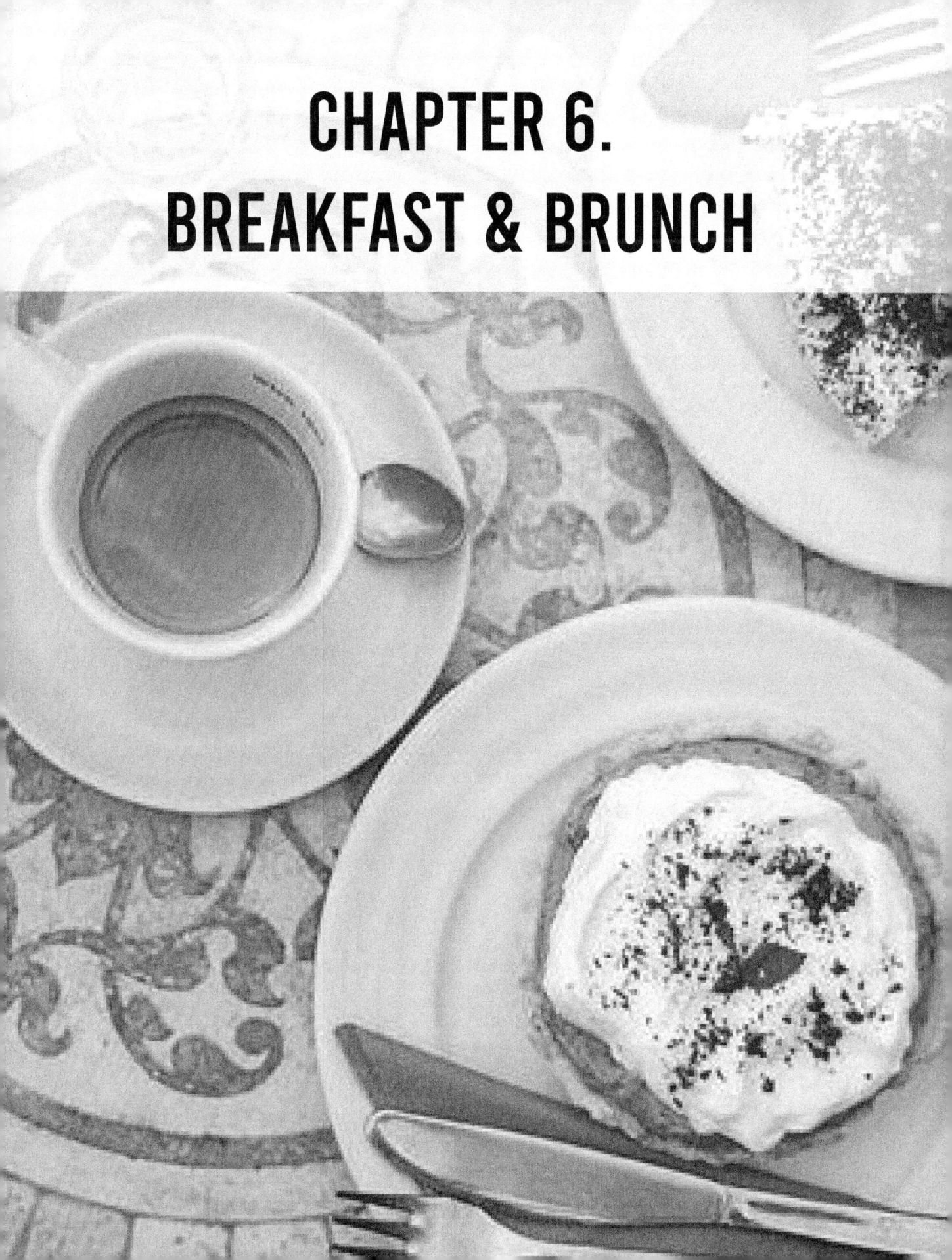

ZUCCHINI CASSEROLE

PREPARATION TIME	COOK TIME	SERVING
15'	3 1/2 H	4

INGREDIENTS

- 2 zucchinis, roughly cubed
- 1 tbsp. almond flour
- 1 egg, beaten
- 1 tsp. ground black pepper
- 1 tsp. coriander, ground
- 1 tsp. oregano, dried
- 1 tsp. basil, dried
- 1 tsp. almond butter, softened
- ½ tsp. salt
- 1/3 cup ground pork, browned
- 1/3 cup coconut milk

DIRECTIONS

- Mix the zucchini with the meat, egg, and the other ingredients.
- Cook the casserole for 3.5 – 4 hours on High.

NUTRIENTS PER SERVING

Calories 303 Fat: 14.3g Carbs: 9.1g Protein: 14.3g

AVOCADO AND ZUCCHINI BAKE

PREPARATION TIME
10'

COOK TIME
2 H

SERVING
8

INGREDIENTS

- 2 avocados, peeled, pitted, and cubed
- 1 zucchini, grated
- 1 tsp. turmeric powder
- 1 tsp. nutmeg, ground
- 3 eggs, beaten
- ½ tsp. almond extract
- ¾ tsp. ground cinnamon
- 1 tbsp. stevia extract
- 1 tsp. butter
- ¾ cup heavy cream

DIRECTIONS

1. Mix the avocado with the zucchini, turmeric, and the other ingredients, stir and spread.
2. Cook egg bake for 2 hours on High.

NUTRIENTS PER SERVING

Calories: 214 Fat: 16.1g Carbs: 9.6g Protein: 10.5g

ALMOND AVOCADO MIX

PREPARATION TIME
15'

COOK TIME
2 H

SERVING
4

INGREDIENTS

- 3 eggs, whisked
- 1 tsp. almond extract
- 1 avocado, peeled, pitted, and mashed
- 1 tbsp. stevia
- 1 cup heavy cream
- ¾ tsp. ground cardamom

DIRECTIONS

1. Mix the eggs with the avocado and the other ingredients.
2. Cook cream bake for 2 hours on High.

NUTRIENTS PER SERVING

Calories: 207 Fat: 7.9g Carbs: 6.6g Protein: 3.2g

BEEF CASSEROLE

PREPARATION TIME
15'

COOK TIME
3 H

SERVING
4

INGREDIENTS

- ½ lb. beef, ground
- 3oz. Mozzarella, shredded
- ½ tsp. sweet paprika
- ½ tsp. chili powder
- ½ tsp. oregano, dried
- 1tbsp. olive oil
- ½ cup coconut milk
- ¼ tsp. cayenne pepper
- ½ tsp. smoked paprika
- ½ tbsp. chives, chopped

DIRECTIONS

1. Heat up a pan with the oil over medium-high heat, add the meat, paprika, chili, and oregano, brown for 5 minutes, and transfer to the slow cooker.
2. Add the rest of the ingredients.
3. Cook the casserole for 3 hours on High.

NUTRIENTS PER SERVING

- Calories: 349 Fat: 20.6g Carbs: 4.4g Protein: 24.5g

SHRIMP CASSEROLE

PREPARATION TIME
10'

COOK TIME
2 H

SERVING
4

INGREDIENTS

- 7 oz. shrimp, cooked and roughly chopped
- ½ cup spring onions, chopped
- 4 eggs, whisked
- 1 tbsp. almond butter, melted
- 1 tsp. paprika
- ½ tsp. chili flakes
- 4 oz. Mozzarella, shredded

DIRECTIONS

1. Brush the slow cooker pot with melted almond butter.
2. Combine the shrimp with spring onions and the other ingredients.
3. Cook the casserole for 2 hours on High.

NUTRIENTS PER SERVING

Calories: 205 Fat: 10.7g Carbs: 3.4g Protein: 11.9g

KETO PORRIDGE

PREPARATION TIME
8'

COOK TIME
2 H

SERVING
3

INGREDIENTS

- 1 tbsp. flaxseed meal
- 3 tbsp. coconut flour
- 1 cup almond milk
- 1 tsp. stevia
- 1 tsp. vanilla extract

DIRECTIONS

1. Place the flaxseed meal, coconut flour, vanilla extract, and stevia in the slow cooker and stir.
2. Add the almond milk and stir.
3. Cook the porridge for 2 hours on low.

NUTRIENTS PER SERVING

Calories: 260 Fat: 21.8g Carbs: 13.3g Protein: 4.3g

SALMON CUTLETS

PREPARATION TIME
15'

COOK TIME
2 H

SERVING
2

INGREDIENTS

- 8 oz. salmon fillet, chopped
- 1 garlic clove, chopped
- 1 oz. onion, chopped
- 1 tbsp. almond flour
- 1 tbsp. coconut flour
- 1/3 tsp. ground black pepper
- ¾ tsp. salt
- 1 tbsp. butter

DIRECTIONS

1. Mix the chopped salmon fillet, garlic, and onion.
2. Add ground black pepper and salt.
3. Add the almond flour and coconut flour.
4. Form medium cutlets from the fish mixture.
5. Put the butter in the slow cooker, then place the fish cutlets in the slow cooker as well.
6. Cook the cutlets for 2 hours on High.

NUTRIENTS PER SERVING

Calories: 305 Fat: 20.2g Carbs: 7.6g Protein: 25.9g

BREAKFAST FRITTATA

PREPARATION TIME
10'

COOK TIME
2-3 H

SERVING
6

INGREDIENTS

- 8 Eggs
- ½ cup cooked sausage
- ¾ spinach, frozen, drained
- ½ tsp. black pepper
- ½ cup chopped onion
- Salt to taste
- ½ cup red bell pepper
- Freezer container
- Freezer bag – 1-gallon size

DIRECTIONS

1. Take a slow cooker and grease its bottom.
2. Mix the frozen spinach, red onion, black pepper, eggs, sausage, and red pepper in the slow cooker.
3. Cook for about 2-3 hours.

NUTRIENTS PER SERVING

Calories: 122 Fat: 9.8g Carbs: 2.5g Protein: 7g.

LEMON PANCAKE

PREPARATION TIME
10'

COOK TIME
1 H

SERVING
4

INGREDIENTS

- 1 tsp. almond extract
- 1 tbsp. stevia
- ½ cup almond flour
- ¾ cup heavy cream
- ½ tsp. baking powder
- 1 tbsp. lemon juice
- 1 tbsp. lemon zest, grated
- 2 eggs, whisked
- 1 tsp. butter, melted

DIRECTIONS

1. Mix the flour with cream, eggs, and the other ingredients except for the butter and mix with a hand mixer.
2. Then place melted butter in the slow cooker.
3. Pour the pancake mixture over the butter and flatten it with the help of a spatula.
4. Cook the pancake for 1 hour on High. You can adjust the time of cooking. It can be from 40 minutes and up to 1.5 hours.

NUTRIENTS PER SERVING

Calories: 201 Fat: 11.2g Carbs: 5.7 Protein: 4g

CINNAMON EGGS

PREPARATION TIME	COOK TIME	SERVING
10'	8 H ON LOW / 2.5 H ON HIGH	4

INGREDIENTS

- 1 tbsp. stevia
- 1 tsp. almond extract
- ½ tsp. ground cinnamon
- 4 eggs, beaten
- 1/3 cup coconut cream
- Cooking spray

DIRECTIONS

1. Combine the eggs with the other ingredients except for the cooking spray.
2. Then spray the slow cooker pot with cooking spray.
3. Transfer the sweet egg mixture to the slow cooker.
4. Cook the breakfast bake for 8 hours on Low or 2.5 hours on High.

NUTRIENTS PER SERVING

Calories: 216 Fat: 11.5g Carbs: 4.9g Protein: 4.8g

DILL AND AVOCADO FRITTATA

PREPARATION TIME
10'

COOK TIME
2 H

SERVING
4

INGREDIENTS

- 2 avocados, peeled, pitted, and mashed
- 1 tsp. green curry paste
- 4 eggs, whisked
- 1 tbsp. fresh dill, chopped
- 1 tsp. butter softened
- 2 oz. Mozzarella, shredded

DIRECTIONS

1. Brush the slow cooker with softened butter from inside.
2. Combine the eggs with avocados and the other ingredients, stir and spread into the pot.
3. Close the lid of the slow cooker and cook the frittata for 2 hours on High.

NUTRIENTS PER SERVING

Calories: 324 Fat 11.7g Carbs: 3.6g Protein: 10.7g

HAM AND KALE BAKE

PREPARATION TIME
10'

COOK TIME
2 H

SERVING
2

INGREDIENTS

- 2 oz. Mozzarella, shredded
- ½ cup kale
- 1 cup ham, chopped
- 1 egg, whisked
- ½ tsp. salt
- ½ tsp. smoked paprika
- ½ tsp. olive oil

DIRECTIONS

1. Brush the slow cooker with the oil from inside.
2. Combine the kale with ham and the other ingredients and spread it into the pan.
3. Close the slow cooker lid and cook the meal for 2 hours on High.

NUTRIENTS PER SERVING

Calories: 235 Fat: 12.3g Carbs: 4.6g Protein: 20.3g

CHILI BAKE

PREPARATION TIME
10'

COOK TIME
8 H

SERVING
6

INGREDIENTS

- 2 green chilies, minced
- 1 ½ cup ground pork
- ½ tsp. salt
- ½ tsp. cayenne pepper
- ¼ tsp. chili powder
- 1 egg, beaten
- 1/3 cup Parmesan cheese, shredded
- ½ onion, chopped
- 1 tbsp. keto tomato sauce
- 1 tbsp. olive oil
- 2 tbsp. chives, chopped

DIRECTIONS

1. Grease the slow cooker with the oil and mix the chilies with the pork and the other ingredients inside.
2. Close the lid and cook the casserole for 8 hours on Low.

NUTRIENTS PER SERVING

Calories: 346 Fat: 10.6g Carbs: 6.2g Protein: 10g

CHEESY BACON CASSEROLE

PREPARATION TIME
10'

COOK TIME
6 H

SERVING
4

INGREDIENTS

- ½ cup Ricotta cheese
- 3 oz. Feta, crumbled
- 3 eggs, whisked
- 3 oz. bacon, chopped
- 1 tsp. olive oil
- 1 tbsp. fresh parsley, chopped
- 1 tbsp. chives, chopped
- 1 tsp. oregano, chopped

DIRECTIONS

1. In the slow cooker, mix the cheese with the eggs and the other ingredients.
2. Stir the casserole gently.
3. Close the slow cooker lid and cook it for 6 hours on Low.

NUTRIENTS PER SERVING

Calories: 353 Fat: 18.2g Carbs: 2.5g Protein: 19g

CREAMY ASPARAGUS BAKE

PREPARATION TIME
10'

COOK TIME
2,5 H

SERVING
6

INGREDIENTS

- 1 cup asparagus, chopped
- 1 cup spring onions, chopped
- ½ cup heavy cream
- 3 oz. Swiss cheese, grated
- 1 tsp. olive oil
- ½ tsp. ground black pepper
- ½ tsp. cayenne pepper
- 1 tsp. dill, chopped

DIRECTIONS

1. In the slow cooker, mix the asparagus with the spring onions and the other ingredients.
2. Stir the baking mixture gently with the help of the wooden spatula.
3. Close the slow cooker lid and cook the casserole for 2.5 hours on High or until the broccoli is tender.

NUTRIENTS PER SERVING

Calories: 250 Fat: 11g Carbs: 4.1g Protein: 9.5g

CAULIFLOWER RICE AND TURKEY CASSEROLE

PREPARATION TIME
10'

COOK TIME
3 H

SERVING
4

INGREDIENTS

- 1 cup cauliflower, diced
- 1 egg, beaten
- 1 cup turkey breast, skinless, boneless, and cut into strips
- ½ tsp. salt
- ½ tsp. smoked paprika
- ¾ tsp. black pepper
- 1 tsp. curry powder
- 1 tbsp. olive oil
- 1 tbsp. Ricotta cheese
- ½ cup heavy cream
- 2 oz. Cheddar cheese, shredded

DIRECTIONS

1. In the slow cooker, mix the rice cauliflower with the turkey and the other ingredients, toss, and close the lid.
2. Cook the meal on High for 3 hours.

NUTRIENTS PER SERVING

Calories: 331 Fat: 13.3g Carbs: 2.5g Protein 11.5g

SAUSAGE AND SPINACH

PREPARATION TIME
15'

COOK TIME
6 H

SERVING
6

INGREDIENTS

- 8 oz. Italian sausages
- 1/3 cup spinach leaves, torn
- 1 tbsp. dried oregano
- 1 tsp. sweet paprika
- 1 tsp. salt
- 1 tsp. black pepper
- 4 oz. Cheddar cheese, shredded
- 1 tbsp. olive oil
- 1/3 cup coconut milk

DIRECTIONS

1. In the slow cooker, mix the sausage with the spinach, oregano, and the other ingredients, toss and close the slow cooker lid.
2. Cook the casserole for 6 hours on Low.

NUTRIENTS PER SERVING

Calories: 377 Fat: 16.4g Carbs: 6.4g Protein: 11.2g

CREAMY EGGS

PREPARATION TIME	COOK TIME	SERVING
10'	7 H	6

INGREDIENTS

- 1 tsp. salt
- 5 eggs, beaten
- ¼ cup heavy cream
- 1 tsp. turmeric powder
- 1 tsp. coriander, ground
- ½ tsp. ground black pepper
- 1 tbsp. fresh parsley, chopped
- ¾ tsp. garlic powder
- ½ tsp. chili flakes
- 1 tbsp. butter
- 4 oz. Mozzarella, shredded
-

DIRECTIONS

1. In the mixing bowl, combine the eggs with the cream and the other ingredients except for the butter and the Mozzarella and whisk.
2. Put the butter in the slow cooker.
3. Add the eggs mix, sprinkle the cheese on top, close the lid, and cook the casserole for 7 hours on Low. The casserole is cooked when the egg mixture is set.

NUTRIENTS PER SERVING

Calories: 301 Fat: 23.8g Carbs: 6.3g Protein: 13.3g

KETO LASAGNA

PREPARATION TIME
20'

COOK TIME
7 H

SERVING
6

INGREDIENTS

- 10 oz. ground beef
- 1 tbsp. tomato puree
- 1 zucchini
- 5 oz. Parmesan, grated
- 1 tbsp. butter
- ½ tsp. salt
- 1 tsp. paprika
- 1 tsp. chili flakes
- 1 tbsp. full-fat heavy cream

DIRECTIONS

1. Mix the ground beef, salt, paprika, and chili flakes.
2. Then mix the full-fat cream and tomato puree.
3. Chop the butter and put it in the slow cooker.
4. Make a layer of the zucchini in the bottom of the slow cooker bowl.
5. Put a layer of the ground beef mixture on top of the zucchini layer.
6. Sprinkle the lasagna with the grated Parmesan.
7. Cook the lasagna for 7 hours on Low.

NUTRIENTS PER SERVING

Calories: 197 Fat: 11g Carbs: 2.5g Protein 22.5g

DUCK BREAST

PREPARATION TIME	COOK TIME	SERVING
10'	5 H	4

INGREDIENTS

- 1 tsp. liquid stevia
- 1lb. duck breast, boneless, skinless
- 1 tsp. chili pepper
- 2 tbsp. butter
- ½ cup water
- 1 bay leaf

DIRECTIONS

1. Rub the duck breast with the chili pepper and liquid stevia, then transfer it to the slow cooker.
2. Add the bay leaf and water.
3. Add butter.
4. Cook the duck breast for 5 hours on Low.
5. Let the cooked duck breast rest for 10 minutes, then remove it from the slow cooker.

NUTRIENTS PER SERVING

Calories: 199 Fat: 10.3g Carbs: 0.3g Protein: 25.1g

CHAPTER 7.
SNACKS AND APPETIZER

BUFFALO MEATBALLS

PREPARATION TIME
5'

COOK TIME
3 H

SERVING
36 MEATBALLS

INGREDIENTS

- 1 cup breadcrumbs
- 2 lb. chicken, ground
- 2 eggs
- ¾ cup buffalo wings sauce
- ½ cup yellow onion, chopped
- 3 garlic cloves, minced
- Salt and black pepper to the taste
- 2 tbsp. olive oil
- ¼ cup butter, melted
- 1 cup blue cheese dressing

DIRECTIONS

1. Mix chicken with breadcrumbs, eggs, onion, garlic, salt, and pepper; stir and shape small meatballs out of this mix.
2. Heat up a pan with the oil over medium-high heat, add meatballs, brown them for a few minutes on each side and transfer them to your Slow Cooker.
3. Add melted butter and buffalo wings sauce, cover, and cook on Low for hours.
4. Arrange meatballs on a platter and serve them with the blue cheese dressing on the side.

NUTRIENTS PER SERVING

Calories: 100 Fat: 7g Carbs: 4g Protein: 4g

SARDINE PATE'

PREPARATION TIME
15'

COOK TIME
3 H

SERVING
6

INGREDIENTS

- ½ cup water
- 3 tbsp. butter
- 1 tsp. onion powder
- 1 tsp. dried parsley
- 12 oz. sardine fillets, chopped

DIRECTIONS

1. Put the chopped sardine fillets, dried parsley, onion powder, and water in the slow cooker.
2. Cook the fish for 3 hours on Low.
3. Strain the sardine fillet.
4. Add butter and blend the mixture for 3 minutes at high speed.

NUTRIENTS PER SERVING

Calories: 170 Fat: 12.3g Carbs: 0.3g Protein 14.1g

GARLICKY BACON SLICES

PREPARATION TIME
5'

COOK TIME
4 H

SERVING
9

INGREDIENTS

- 10 oz. Canadian bacon, sliced
- 2 tbsp. garlic powder
- 2 garlic cloves, peeled and sliced
- 2 tbsp. whipped cream
- 1 tsp. dried dill
- 1 tsp. chili flakes
- ½ tsp. salt

DIRECTIONS

1. Season the bacon with garlic powder and spread it in the Slow Cooker.
2. Whisk the cream with garlic, dill, salt, and chili flakes in a bowl.
3. Spread this cream mixture over the bacon strips and leave for 10 minutes.
4. Put the cooker's lid on and set the cook time to 3 hours on High settings.
5. Flip the bacon slices and remove excess liquid out of the cooker.
6. Put the cooker's lid on and set the cook time to 1 hour on High settings.
7. Serve.

NUTRIENTS PER SERVING

Calories: 51g Fat: 1.6g Carbs: 2.60g Protein: 7g

BACON FINGERLING POTATOES

PREPARATION TIME
5'

COOK TIME
8 H

SERVING
15

INGREDIENTS

- 2 lb. fingerling potatoes
- 8 oz. bacon
- 1 tsp. onion powder
- 1 tsp. chili powder
- 1 tsp. garlic powder
- 1 tsp. paprika
- 3 tbsp. butter
- 1 tsp. dried dill
- 1 tbsp. rosemary

DIRECTIONS

1. Grease the base of your Slow Cooker with butter.
2. Spread the fingerling potatoes in the buttered cooker.
3. Mix all the spices, herbs, and bacon in a bowl.
4. Spread bacon-spice mixture over the lingering potatoes.
5. Put the cooker's lid on and set the cooking time to 8 hours on Low settings.
6. Serve warm.

NUTRIENTS PER SERVING

Calories: 117 Fat: 6.9g Carbs: 12g Protein: 3g

TACO DIP

PREPARATION TIME
5'

COOK TIME
2 H

SERVING
4

INGREDIENTS

- ½ rotisserie chicken, shredded
- 1 cup pepper jack, cheese, grated
- 8oz. canned enchilada sauce
- ½ jalapeno, sliced
- 4 oz. cream cheese, soft
- ½ tbsp. taco seasoning

DIRECTIONS

1. In your Slow Cooker, mix chicken with pepper jack, enchilada sauce, jalapeno, cream, and taco seasoning, stir, cover, and cook on High for an hour.
2. Stir the dip, cover, and cook on Low for 1 hour and 30 minutes more.
3. Divide into bowls and serve as a snack.

NUTRIENTS PER SERVING

Calories: 259 Fat: 7g Carbs: 18g Protein: 9g

SPINACH MUSSELS SALAD

PREPARATION TIME
5'

COOK TIME
1 H

SERVING
4

INGREDIENTS

- 2 lb. mussels, cleaned and scrubbed
- 1 radicchio, cut into thin strips
- 1 white onion, chopped
- 1 lb. baby spinach
- ½ cup dry white wine
- 1 garlic clove, crushed
- ½ cup of water
- A drizzle of olive oil

DIRECTIONS

1. Add mussels, onion, water, oil, garlic, and wine to the Slow Cooker.
2. Put the cooker's lid on and set the cooking time to 1 hour on High settings.
3. Spread the radicchio and spinach in the serving plates.
4. Divide the cooked mussels over the spinach leaves.
5. Serve.

NUTRIENTS PER SERVING

Calories: 59 Fat: 4g Carbs: 1g Protein: 1g

CASHEW DIP

PREPARATION TIME
5'

COOK TIME
3 H

SERVING
10

INGREDIENTS

- 1 cup water
- 1 cup cashews
- 10 oz. hummus
- ¼ tsp. garlic powder
- ¼ tsp. onion powder
- A pinch of salt and black pepper
- ¼ tsp. mustard powder
- 1 tsp. apple cider vinegar

DIRECTIONS

1. In your Slow Cooker, mix water with cashews, salt, and pepper, stir, cover, and cook on High for 3 hours.
2. Transfer to your blender, add hummus, garlic powder, onion powder, mustard powder, and vinegar, pulse well, divide into bowls and serve.

NUTRIENTS PER SERVING

Calories: 192 Fat: 7g Carbs: 12g Protein 4g

BLUE CHEESE PARSLEY DIP

PREPARATION TIME
5'

COOK TIME
7 H

SERVING
7

INGREDIENTS

- 1 cup parsley, chopped
- 8 oz. celery stalk, chopped
- 6 oz. Blue cheese, chopped
- 1 tbsp. apple cider vinegar
- 6 oz. cream
- 1 tsp. minced garlic
- 1 tsp. paprika
- ¼ tsp. ground red pepper
- 1 onion, peeled and grated

DIRECTIONS

1. Whisk the cream with cream cheese in a bowl and add to the Slow Cooker.
2. Toss in parsley, celery stalk, garlic, onion, apple cider vinegar, and red pepper ground.
3. Put the cooker's lid on and set the cooking time to 7 hours on Low settings.
4. Mix the dip after hours of cooking, then resume cooked.
5. Serve.

NUTRIENTS PER SERVING

Calories: 151 Fat: 11.9g Carbs: 5.14g Protein: 7g

BROCCOLI DIP

PREPARATION TIME
5'

COOK TIME
2 H

SERVING
2

INGREDIENTS

- 1 green chili pepper, minced
- 2 tbsp. heavy cream
- 1 cup broccoli florets
- 1 tbsp. mayonnaise
- 2 tbsp. cream cheese, cubed
- A pinch of salt and black pepper
- 1 tbsp. chives, chopped

DIRECTIONS

1. In your Slow Cooker, mix the broccoli with the chili pepper, mayo, and the other ingredients, toss, put the lid on and cook on Low for 2 hours.
2. Blend using an immersion blender, divide into bowls and serve as a party dip.

NUTRIENTS PER SERVING

Calories: 202 Fat: 3g Carbs: 7g Protein 6g

CHOCO ROASTED ALMONDS

PREPARATION TIME
5'

COOK TIME
3 H

SERVING
2

INGREDIENTS

- 2 tbsp. raw almonds
- 1 tsp. unsweetened dark cocoa powder
- 1 tsp. Stevia powder
- 1 pinch of Himalayan salt

DIRECTIONS

1. Grease your slow cooker. Place the roasted almonds in a bowl and add the cocoa powder and Stevia powder. Combine well and place in the slow cooker
2. Set on high and cook for 3 hours stirring every 30 minutes.
3. Let almonds cool before serving.
4. Store in a seal-able container for up to 6 months.

NUTRIENTS PER SERVING

Calories: 196 Fat: 15.8g Carbs: 7.6 Protein: 6.8g

HONEY CHICKEN WINGS

PREPARATION TIME
10'

COOK TIME
6 1/2 - 7 H

SERVING
2

INGREDIENTS

- 1,5 lb. chicken wings
- ½ cup honey
- 1 tbsp. olive oil
- ¼ soy sauce, low sodium
- 1 clove garlic, minced

DIRECTIONS

1. In a bowl mix well soy sauce, oil, honey and garlic.
2. Place chicken wings in the slow cooker and pour the sauce mixture, until the chicken wings are well coated with the sauce mixture.
3. Set on Low and cook for 6.5/7 hours

NUTRIENTS PER SERVING

calories: 416, fat: 24, carbs: 16.9, protein 31.5g

GLAZED WALNUTS

PREPARATION TIME	COOK TIME	SERVING
10'	2 H	8

INGREDIENTS

- 8 oz. walnuts halves
- ¼ cup maple syrup
- ¼ cup butter, unsalted
- ½ tsp. vanilla extract

DIRECTIONS

1. Mix a bowl all ingredients and combine until well mixed.
2. Place in the slow cooker, set on Low and cook for 2 hours, checking and stirring for walnuts are well coated.
3. Let the walnuts cool before serving.

NUTRIENTS PER SERVING

calories: 245, fat: 25g, carbs: 10g, protein 4.2g

KETO CHOCOLATE PUDDING

PREPARATION TIME
5'

COOK TIME
2 1/2 - 3 H

SERVING
2

INGREDIENTS

- 2 cups coconut milk
- 2 tbsp. Erythritol
- 1tbsp. bitter cocoa powder
- 1tsp. glucomannan powder

DIRECTIONS

1. Combine milk with cocoa and sweetener
2. Slowly, to avoid lumps, join glucomannan
3. Grease the slow cooker, and place the mixture using a spoon.
4. Set on High and cook for 3 hours.

NUTRIENTS PER SERVING

calories: 400, fat: 20.3g, carbs: 12g, protein 3.25g

GOAT CHEESE DUMPLINGS

PREPARATION TIME
5'

COOK TIME
4 H

SERVING
6

INGREDIENTS

- ¼ cup of goat cheese
- 2 tbsp. pistachios, finely chopped
- 2 tbsp. almonds, finely chopped
- Thai spices or other spices to taste

DIRECTIONS

1. Grease the slow cooker.
2. Cut cheese into 6 pieces and form balls
3. Insert pistachios and almonds into a vacuum bag
4. Add salt, pepper and spices to the bag.
5. Spread the mixture on a plate and roll in it your cheese balls before putting them in the slow cooker.
6. Set on Low and cook for 4 hours.

NUTRIENTS PER SERVING

calories: 350, fat: 29g, carbs: 9g, protein 17.3g

GARLICKY NUGGETS

PREPARATION TIME
20'

COOK TIME
2 H

SERVING
10

INGREDIENTS

- 28 oz. little smoked sausage links
- ½ cup Ketchup
- 1/3 cup honey
- ¼ cup brown sugar
- 2 tbsp. soy sauce, low sodium
- 4 cloves garlic, minced

DIRECTIONS

1. In a bowl combine well all ingredients except the smoked sausage.
2. Place the little sausages in the slow cooker and pour over the sauce, toss until well coated.
3. Set on High and cook for 2 hours.
4. Serve warm.

NUTRIENTS PER SERVING

calories: 320, fat: 22g, carbs: 18.9g, protein 11g

LEMON ASPARAGUS

PREPARATION TIME
5'

COOK TIME
2 H

SERVING
8

INGREDIENTS

- 1 bunch asparagus, rinsed and trimmed
- 3 lemon slices
- 1 cup fresh lemon juice
- 1 water
- 1 clove garlic, minced
- ½ tsp. salt
- Black pepper to taste

DIRECTIONS

1. Combine all ingredients in a bowl until well mixed.
2. Place asparagus in the slow cooker and pour the sauce mixture on the top.
3. Set on High and cook for 1.5/2 hours.
4. Top with lemon slices before serving.

NUTRIENTS PER SERVING

calories: 79, fat: 2.6g, carbs: 14g, protein 2g

CHAPTER 8.
FISH AND SEAFOOD

SEAFOOD STEW

PREPARATION TIME
5'

COOK TIME
8 H

SERVING
6

INGREDIENTS

- 2 tbsp. fresh parsley
- 1/2 tsp. salt
- 1 tsp.dried basil leaves
- 1/4 tsp. red pepper sauce
- 2 tbsp. olive oil
- 1 cup baby carrots
- 3 cups sliced quartered Roma tomatoes
- 1 tsp.Splenda
- 1/2 cup green bell pepper
- 1 cup water
- 1/2 tsp. fennel seed
- 1/2 lb. peeled and deveined shrimp
- 1lb. cod
- 2 garlic cloves

DIRECTIONS

1. Mix garlic and oil. Add tomatoes, carrots, fennel seed, bell pepper, clam juice, and water.
2. Cook for 8 to 9 hours on low heat.

NUTRIENTS PER SERVING

Calories: 118 Fat: 5.8g Carbs: 4.7g Protein: 25g

SLOW COOKED SHRIMP

PREPARATION TIME
5'

COOK TIME
4 H

SERVING
4

INGREDIENTS

- 1 1/2 cup shrimp
- 1 can cream of shrimp soup
- 2 egg yolks
- 4 oz. mushrooms
- 3/4 evaporated milk

DIRECTIONS

1. Put all ingredients except the egg yolks in the slow cooker.
2. Cook for 4 to 5 hours on low.
3. Add the egg yolks, then cook for another hour.

NUTRIENTS PER SERVING

Calories: 194 Fat: 9g Carbs: 9g Protein: 17g

TUNA AND WHITE BEANS SALAD

PREPARATION TIME
5'

COOK TIME
9 H

SERVING
6

INGREDIENTS

- 4 tbsp.extra virgin olive oil
- 1 garlic clove
- 1 lb.white beans
- 6 cups water
- 14 oz. canned white tuna in water
- 2 cups tomatoes
- 2 tsp. dried basil
- Salt and pepper
- 1 bunch Romaine lettuce

DIRECTIONS

1. Add olive oil to a skillet.
2. Sauté the garlic for 1 minute.
3. Remove the garlic from the pan.
4. Cook the beans in the slow cooker on low for 3 hours.
5. Add the garlic-flavored olive oil.
6. Pour the water into the pot.
7. Cover and set it on high—cook for 1 hour.
8. Reduce the temperature to low.
9. Cook for another 5 hours.
10. Add the tuna, tomatoes, and basil.

NUTRIENTS PER SERVING

Calories: 468 Fat: 15.5g Protein: 35.8g Carbs: 46g

SHRIMP CREOLE

PREPARATION TIME
5'

COOK TIME
4 H

SERVING
6

INGREDIENTS

- 1 cup onion
- 1 garlic clove
- 1 cup red bell pepper
- 1 cup celery
- 1 tsp. salt
- 1/4 tsp. pepper
- 6 drops Tabasco
- 1/2 tsp. Creole seasoning
- 4 oz. canned tomato sauce
- 14 oz. canned whole tomatoes

- 2 lb. shrimp
- 1/2 cup white rice

DIRECTIONS

1. Add all the ingredients to the slow cooker, except for the shrimp.
2. Cook on High for 4 hours.
3. In the last 30 minutes of your cooking, add the shrimp.

NUTRIENTS PER SERVING

calories: 309, fat: 3g, protein: 35g, carbs: 28g

SALMON AND SCALLOPED POTATOES

PREPARATION TIME
5'

COOK TIME
9 H

SERVING
9

INGREDIENTS

- Cooking spray
- 3 tbsp. flour
- Salt and pepper
- 16 oz. salmon
- 5 potatoes
- 1/2 cup onion
- 1/4 cup water
- 10 oz. cream of mushroom soup
- Pinch of nutmeg

DIRECTIONS

1. Grease your slow cooker with cooking spray.
2. Sprinkle with a little bit of flour.
3. Sprinkle with salt and pepper.
4. Arrange a layer of half of the salmon flakes, half of the potatoes, and half of the chopped onions.
5. Make another set of layers.
6. Mix the water and soup.
7. Pour into the slow cooker. Add the nutmeg.
8. Cover the pot. Cook on low for 9 hours.

NUTRIENTS PER SERVING

Calories: 174 Fat: 4.2g Protein: 12.4g Carbs: 22g

TILAPIA IN LEMON PEPPER SAUCE

PREPARATION TIME
5'

COOK TIME
2 H

SERVING
4

INGREDIENTS

- 4 fillets tilapia
- 16 spears asparagus
- 8 tbsp. freshly squeezed lemon juice
- 8 tbsp. pepper
- 2 tbsp.butter

DIRECTIONS

1. Cut the foil.
2. Put each tilapia fillet into the foil.
3. Place 4 spears of asparagus on each tilapia.
4. Sprinkle each fillet with ¼ tsp. pepper.
5. Sprinkle 2 tbsp. lemon juice onto each fillet.
6. Add ½ tbsp. butter on each fillet.
7. Wrap the fillet with the foil.
8. Place wrapped tilapia in the slow cooker.
9. Cook on High for 2 hours.

NUTRIENTS PER SERVING

Calories: 172 Fat: 7.2g Protein: 23.6g Carbs: 4.7g

ASIAN STYLE SALMON

PREPARATION TIME	COOK TIME	SERVING
5'	3 H	4

INGREDIENTS

- 16 oz. frozen veggies
- Salt and pepper
- 10 oz. salmon fillets
- 2 tbsp. lemon juice
- 2 tbsp. soy sauce
- 2 tbsp. honey
- 1 tsp. sesame honey
- 1 tsp. sesame seeds

DIRECTIONS

1. Put the vegetables on a slow cooker.
2. Rub the salt and pepper on to the salmon fillets.
3. Put the salmon fillets on top of the vegetables.
4. Combine the lemon juice, soy sauce, and honey.
5. Pour this mixture over the salmon.
6. Sprinkle with sesame seeds.
7. Set cooker to low. Cook for 3 hours.

NUTRIENTS PER SERVING

Calories: 210 Fat: 5g Protein: 18g Carbs 23g

SHRIMP SCAMPI

PREPARATION TIME
5'

COOK TIME
2 H

SERVING
4

INGREDIENTS

- 1/2 cup white wine
- 1/4 cup reduced sodium chicken stock
- 2 tbsp. freshly squeezed lemon juice
- 2 tsp.parsley
- 2 tsp. garlic
- 2 tbsp. olive oil
- 1 lb. large shrimp

DIRECTIONS

1. Mix all the ingredients.
2. Transfer to the slow cooker.
3. Cook on low for 2 hours.

NUTRIENTS PER SERVING

Calories: 180 Fat: 7.1g Protein: 21.5g Carbs 3.5g

POACHED SALMON WITH LEMONS

PREPARATION TIME
12'

COOK TIME
1 H

SERVING
8

INGREDIENTS

- 2 lb. salmon
- 1 cup water
- 1 cup dry white wine
- 1 lemon
- 1 celery rib
- 1 fennel bulb.
- 1 bay leaf
- 1 tsp. salt
- 1 tsp. pepper
- ½ tsp. red pepper flakes

DIRECTIONS

1. Mix: water, white wine, lemon, chopped celery rib, and chopped fennel bulb, bay leaf, and a half of salt. Pour this mixture in the slow cooker and let it simmer for half an hour.
2. Let this cook on high for another 45-60 minutes.

NUTRIENTS PER SERVING

Calories: 204 Fat: 7.5g Fiber: 0.6g Carbs: 1.5g Protein 16g

GARLIC SHRIMPS

PREPARATION TIME	COOK TIME	SERVING
12'	1 H	8

INGREDIENTS

- 2 lb. raw shrimp
- ½ cup extra-virgin olive oil
- ¼ cup dry sherry
- 2 tbsp.squeezed lemon juice
- 6 cloves garlic
- 1 bell pepper
- 1 tsp.sea salt
- 1 tsp. spicy curry powder
- ¼ tsp. chipotle powder
- ¼ tsp. freshly ground white pepper
- 1 tbsp. parsley
- 1 tbsp. dill

DIRECTIONS

1. Mix in the olive oil, dry sherry, lemon juice, garlic, bell pepper, salt, curry powder, chipotle powder, and white pepper. Let it simmer on high for half an hour.
2. Add the shrimps and cook everything for 10 minutes.
3. Cook for another 10 minutes.

NUTRIENTS PER SERVING

Calories: 301 Fat: 20.8g Fiber: 0.1 g Carbs: 2.6g Protein: 26g

CHILI SHRIMPS

PREPARATION TIME
15'

COOK TIME
2 H

SERVING
6

INGREDIENTS

- 2 tbsp. avocado oil
- 1 ½ lb. medium raw shrimps
- ½ tsp.kosher salt
- ½ tsp. curry powder
- ½tsp.red pepper flakes
- ½ tsp.pepper
- ½ tsp. coriander powder
- 2 tbsp. dried celery flakes
- 2 large ripe tomatoes
- 2 red bell peppers

- 1 chili pepper
- 2 cloves garlic, minced
- 1 tbsp.Sirach hot sauce
- 1 lb. fire roasted tomatoes

DIRECTIONS

1. Drizzle the pot with a generous amount of avocado oil.
2. Place the shrimps on the pot.
3. Add spices.
4. Mix the following: diced tomatoes, red bell peppers, chili pepper, garlic, and Sirach hot sauce. Pour this mixture in the slow cooker. Top with fire roasted tomatoes.
5. Cook on high for 2 hours.

NUTRIENTS PER SERVING

Calories: 185 Fat: 6.7g Fiber: 2.2g Carbs: 5.2g Protein 28.4g

HEARTY WHITE FISH STEW

PREPARATION TIME	COOK TIME	SERVING
15'	6 H	6

INGREDIENTS

- 1 ½ lb. white fish
- 2 tbsp. butter
- 1 lb. tomatoes
- 1 to 2 small zucchini
- 1 large clove garlic
- 1 large onion
- 1 green bell pepper
- ½ tsp. dried basil
- ½ tsp.dried oregano
- 1 tsp.salt
- ⅛ tsp.pepper
- ¼ cup fish stock

DIRECTIONS

1. Stir everything together in the slow cooker pot.
2. Cook on high for 5-6 hours.

NUTRIENTS PER SERVING

Calories: 168 Fat: 6.8g Carbs: 4.5g Protein: 16.4g

SEAFOOD STEW

PREPARATION TIME
15'

COOK TIME
2 1/2 H

SERVING
8

INGREDIENTS

- 2 lb. seafood, a variety of squid, shrimps
- 4 cups tomatoes
- 4 cups seafood stock
- ½ cup dry sherry
- 4 medium celery stalks
- 2 cloves garlic
- 1 tsp. kosher salt
- 1 tsp. dried chives
- 1 tsp. dried celery flakes
- ½ tsp. dried marjoram
- ½ tsp. dried oregano
- ¼ tsp. pepper
- ¼ tsp. smoked paprika
- ¼ tsp. chipotle powder
- 2 tbsp. fresh basil to serve

DIRECTIONS

1. Mix the following: diced tomatoes, seafood stock, dry sherry, chopped celery, garlic, salt, dried chives, dried celery flakes, dried marjoram, dried oregano, white pepper, smoked paprika, and chipotle powder.
2. Let it simmer for 2 hours.
3. Add the seafood mix and cook it on high for another half an hour.

NUTRIENTS PER SERVING

Calories: 196 Fat: 2.8g Carbs: 6.1g Protein: 19.4g

SEAFOOD BOWLS

PREPARATION TIME
10'

COOK TIME
3 H

SERVING
4

INGREDIENTS

- 5 oz. scallops
- 4 oz. shrimps
- ½ lb. salmon
- 1 tsp. lemongrass
- 1 tsp. salt
- 1 tsp. cayenne pepper
- 1/3 cup crushed tomatoes
- 1 tsp. cumin seeds
- 1 tbsp. avocado oil
- 1 tsp. smoked paprika

- 1 oz. fennel bulb.
- 1 tsp. lemon rind
- 1 tsp. onion powder
- ½ cup water

DIRECTIONS

1. Preheat the skillet well and add olive oil.
2. Add fennel and the other ingredients except the seafood, stir, cook for 5 minutes.
3. Add remaining ingredients, cook on High for 1 hour and Low for 2 hours.

NUTRIENTS PER SERVING

Calories: 246 Fat: 5g Carbs: 5g Protein 21g

SALMON SOUP

PREPARATION TIME
8'

COOK TIME
3 H

SERVING
4

INGREDIENTS

- 2 cups water
- 1 cup coconut cream
- 1 tsp. garlic powder
- 2 garlic cloves
- 1 tsp. lemongrass
- ½ tsp. chili flakes
- 8 oz. salmon
- 1 tsp. salt

DIRECTIONS

1. Mix the water with cream and the other ingredients except the fish.
2. Cook the stock for 2 hours on High.
3. Add salmon.
4. Cook the soup for 1 hour on Low.

NUTRIENTS PER SERVING

Calories: 209 Fat: 12g Carbs: 5g Protein 7g

SHRIMP BAKE

PREPARATION TIME	COOK TIME	SERVING
10'	2 H	2

INGREDIENTS

- 1lb. shrimp
- 2 tbsp. lime juice
- 1 tsp. salt
- 1 tsp. apple cider vinegar
- 1 tbsp. butter
- ¾ cup heavy cream
- 2oz. provolone cheese

DIRECTIONS

1. Mix the shrimp with the lime juice and the other ingredients except the cheese.
2. Toss, sprinkle the cheese on top and cook on High for 2 hours.

NUTRIENTS PER SERVING

Calories: 290 Fat: 5g Carbs: 3g Protein: 18g

SHRIMP AND SALMON SKEWERS

PREPARATION TIME
10'

COOK TIME
2 H

SERVING
4

INGREDIENTS

- 9 oz. shrimps
- 9 oz. salmon fillets
- 1 tsp. garlic powder
- 1 tsp. ginger powder
- 1 tbsp. lime juice
- 1/3 tsp. oregano
- 1 tbsp. sesame oil
- 1 tsp. heavy cream
- ¾ cup water

DIRECTIONS

1. String the shrimps and salmon into the skewers one-by-one.
2. Pour water.
3. Add the rest of the ingredients as well.
4. Cook shrimps for 1.5 hours on High.

NUTRIENTS PER SERVING

Calories: 185 Fat: 5g Carbs: 5g Protein: 14g

SHRIMP SALAD

PREPARATION TIME	COOK TIME	SERVING
10'	30 MIN	4

INGREDIENTS

- ¼ cup cherry tomatoes
- 1 cup kale
- ½ cup avocado
- 7 oz. shrimps
- 1 tsp. basil
- 3 tbsp. butter
- 1 tbsp. olive oil
- 1 tbsp. parsley
- ¾ cup heavy cream
- 1 tsp. ground black pepper
- ½ tsp. salt

DIRECTIONS

1. Mix the shrimp with tomatoes and the other ingredients.
2. Cook for 30 minutes on High.

NUTRIENTS PER SERVING

Calories: 248 Fat: 11g Carbs: 2g Protein: 8g

FLAVORED TILAPIA

PREPARATION TIME
10'

COOK TIME
2 H

SERVING
4

INGREDIENTS

- 1 asparagus bunch, spears trimmed
- 12 tbsp. lemon juice
- 4 tilapia fillets
- A pinch of lemon pepper
- 2 tbsp. olive oil

DIRECTIONS

1. Divide tilapia fillets on 4 parchment paper pieces.
2. Divide asparagus on top, drizzle the lemon juice, and sprinkle a pinch of pepper.
3. Drizzle the oil all over, wrap fish and asparagus, and place in your slow cooker.
4. Cover and cook on High for 2 hours.

NUTRIENTS PER SERVING

Calories: 200 Fat: 3g Fiber: 1g Carbs: 8g Protein: 6g

SPECIAL SEAFOOD CHOWDER

PREPARATION TIME
10'

COOK TIME
8 HOURS 30 MIN

SERVING
4

INGREDIENTS

- 2 cups water
- ½ fennel bulb, chopped
- 2 sweet potatoes, cubed
- 1 yellow onion, chopped
- 2 bay leaves
- 1 tbsp. thyme, dried
- 1 celery rib, chopped
- Black pepper to the taste
- A pinch of cayenne pepper
- 1 bottle clam juice

- 2 tbsp. tapioca powder
- 1 cup coconut milk
- 1 lb. salmon fillets, cubed
- 5 sea scallops, halved
- 24 shrimp, peeled and deveined
- ¼ cup parsley, chopped

DIRECTIONS

1. In your slow cooker, mix water with fennel, potatoes, onion, bay leaves, thyme, celery, clam juice, cayenne, black pepper, and tapioca powdered, stir, cover, and cook on Low for 8 hours.
2. Add salmon, coconut milk, scallops, shrimp, and parsley, cover, and cook on Low for 30 minutes more.

NUTRIENTS PER SERVING

Calories: 354 Fat: 10g Fiber: 2g Carbs: 10g Protein: 12g

CHAPTER 9.
POULTRY

CHEESE-STUFFED TURKEY MEATBALLS

PREPARATION TIME
5'

COOK TIME
6 H

SERVING
8

INGREDIENTS

- 2 tbsp. Italian seasonings
- ½ cup Grated parmesan cheese
- ½ cup Rolled oats
- 2 eggs
- Pepper to taste
- Salt to taste
- ½ Garlic powder
- 8 oz. Fontina cheese
- 2 ½ lb. turkey
- Marinara Sauce Ingredients:
- 1 can (28 oz.) tomatoes
- 1 tbsp. EVO
- ½ tsp. pepper
- 1 tsp. of each:
- Salt
- Parsley
- Dried basil
- Garlic

DIRECTIONS

1. Whisk the cheese, eggs, oats, and seasonings.
2. Fold in the turkey and roll into 24 meatballs.
3. Insert one tube of the cheese in the middle of each turkey meatballs.
4. Prepare the marinara sauce, and pour a layer into the cooker. Place the meatballs in the sauce, and stir in the remainder of the sauce.
5. Prepare for six hours using the lowest setting.

NUTRIENTS PER SERVING

Calories: 345 Fat: 18g Carbs: 4.5g Protein: 35g

BUTTER CHICKEN

PREPARATION TIME	COOK TIME	SERVING
15'	3 H	4

INGREDIENTS

- 4 tbsp. butter
- 3 oz. spinach, chopped
- 1 tsp. onion powder
- 1 tsp. paprika
- 12 oz. chicken breast, skinless, boneless
- ½ tsp. salt
- ¼ cup chicken stock

DIRECTIONS

1. Beat the chicken breasts and sprinkle them with the salt and paprika.
2. Place the butter and spinach in a blender.
3. Add onion powder and blend the mixture for 1 minute at high speed.
4. Spread the chicken breast with the butter mixture on each side.
5. Place the buttered chicken in the slow cooker and the chicken stock.
6. Cook the chicken for 3 hours on Low.

NUTRIENTS PER SERVING

Calories: 208 Fat: 13.9g Carbs: 1.6g Protein: 18.9g

CREAMY TUSCAN CHICKEN

PREPARATION TIME
15'

COOK TIME
7 H

SERVING
8

INGREDIENTS

- 1lb. chicken breast, skinless, boneless
- 1 tbsp. olive oil
- ½ cup full-fat cream
- 1 oz. spinach, chopped
- 3 oz. Parmesan, grated
- 1 tsp. chili flakes
- ½ tsp. paprika
- 1 tsp. minced garlic
- ½ tsp. ground black pepper

DIRECTIONS

1. Chop the chicken breast and sprinkle it with the chili flakes, paprika, minced garlic, and ground black pepper.
2. Stir the chicken and transfer it to the slow cooker.
3. Add the full-fat cream and olive oil.
4. Add spinach and grated cheese.
5. Cook the chicken for 7 hours on Low.

NUTRIENTS PER SERVING

Calories: 136 Fat: 7.2g Carbs: 1.4g Protein 16g

CHICKEN LEGS

PREPARATION TIME
5'

COOK TIME
6 H

SERVING
12

INGREDIENTS

- 2 cup water
- 2 tbsp. swerve/15 drops stevia drops
- ¼ cup liquid amino
- Optional: ¼ tsp. blackstrap molasses
- Garlic powder
- Ground ginger
- Pepper and salt to taste
- 6 ½ lb. chicken thighs & drumsticks

DIRECTIONS

1. Mix the molasses, amino, sweetener, garlic powder, water, and ground ginger. Cut the chicken up into pieces.
2. Prepare the chicken on the high setting for five to six hours.

NUTRIENTS PER SERVING

Calories: 587 Fat: 42.8g Carbs: 0.7g Protein: 53.5g

CHICKEN LO MEIN

PREPARATION TIME
5'

COOK TIME
4 H

SERVING
6

INGREDIENTS

- ½ tsp. minced garlic paste
- ½ tsp. sesame oil
- 1 tbsp. coconut or soy Amino/tamari
- 1 ½ lb. chicken
- 12 oz. Noodles
- 1 tsp. minced ginger
- 1 bunch Napa cabbage/Bok choy
- 2 minced garlic cloves
- 2 tsp. sesame oil
- ¾ cup chicken broth

- ¼ cup tamari/Soy or Coconut amino
- Rice vinegar
- Sukrin Gold Fiber Syrup/favorite sweetener
- 1 tsp. red pepper chili flakes
- ½ tsp. xanthan gum – thickener

DIRECTIONS

1. Remove all skin and bones from the chicken. Combine and place the chicken and marinate in the fridge for about thirty minutes.
2. Spray the cooker with some cooking oil spray. Add the chicken and cook for one to two hours on the low setting.
3. Add the Chinese cabbage, ginger, and garlic in the cooker. Arrange the chicken on top. Make the sauce fixings and add over the top of the chicken.
4. Cook using the low heat setting for about 1 ½-2 hours or 30 minutes to one hour on high.
5. Make the noodles ten minutes before the cooking cycle is done by rinsing and soaking them in water. Use tongs to blend in the noodles and cover with the sauce. Add the thickener if needed.
6. Change the temperature to high and continue cooking for another 10-15 minutes.

NUTRIENTS PER SERVING

Calories: 175 Fat: 8g Carbs: 1.5g Protein: 24.5g

CHIPOTLE GARLIC & LIME CHICKEN

PREPARATION TIME
5'

COOK TIME
6 H

SERVING
6

INGREDIENTS

- 1 ½ lb. chicken thighs/breasts
- Sauce Ingredients:
- 3 tbsp. lime juice
- 1/3 cup tomato sauce
- 1 tbsp. apple cider vinegar
- 2 tbsp. each:
- Canned mild green chilies
- Avocado/olive oil
- 2 -3 cloves of garlic
- 1/3 cup cilantro
- 1 ½ tsp. swerve/coconut sugar
- ½-1 tsp. mild to spicy ground chipotle powder
- ¼ tsp. black pepper
- 1 tsp. sea salt

DIRECTIONS

1. Add the chicken to the slow cooker and the sauce.
2. Prepare the cooker for six to eight hours on low or high for four to six hours.

NUTRIENTS PER SERVING

Calories: 189 Fat: 9g Carbs: 7g Protein 22g

COCONUT BASIL CURRY CHICKEN

PREPARATION TIME
5'

COOK TIME
8 H

SERVING
6

INGREDIENTS

- 1 jalapeno
- 1 onion
- 6 thighs
- 1 can – 13½ oz. coconut milk
- 2 tbsp. coconut oil
- 1 tbsp. Grated fresh ginger
- 1 tbsp. Minced garlic
- 1 tbsp. Curry powder
- 1 tsp. sea salt
- 2 tsp. tapioca starch

- 1 small juiced lime
- 15-20 basil leaves

DIRECTIONS

1. Arrange the thighs in the slow cooker and add the milk. Set the timer for four hours on high.
2. About 1 hour before the cooking cycle is complete, pour the oil into a saucepan on the stovetop. Toss in the onion and jalapeno. Sauté for three minutes.
3. Blend in the tapioca, curry powder, garlic, salt, and ginger. Stir for about 30 seconds.
4. Cook another 45 minutes. Shred the chicken. Stir in the basil and juice until well combined.

NUTRIENTS PER SERVING

Calories: 467 Fat: 39g Protein: 20g Carbs: 9g Fiber: 3.8 g

CREAMY STYLE BACON & CHEESE CHICKEN

PREPARATION TIME
5'

COOK TIME
4 H

SERVING
8

INGREDIENTS

- 4-6 chicken breasts
- 3 tbsp. butter
- ¾ cup chicken broth
- ½ tsp. each:
- Rosemary
- Poultry seasoning
- ¼ tsp. thyme
- 1 tsp. garlic
- 6 bacon slices
- ⅔ cup heavy whipping cream

- 2 oz. cream cheese
- 1 cup cheddar cheese
- ¾ tsp. xanthan gum
- Pepper and salt to taste
- Cooking oil spray

DIRECTIONS

1. Arrange the chicken in the slow cooker. Mix in the butter, poultry seasoning, rosemary, thyme, garlic, and the chicken broth.
2. Crumble three pieces of cooked bacon, and cook on the high setting for 3- 3 ½ hours.
3. Pour in the cream along with a dollop of cheese. Stir well to combine.
4. Use two forks to shred the chicken. Sprinkle with the xanthan gum, and let it simmer for a few minutes to thicken.
5. Grease the casserole dish, and add the contents. Sprinkle with the cup of cheese, and crumble the last of the bacon bits on top.
6. Place the casserole dish in the oven on the broil setting for 2-4 minutes.

NUTRIENTS PER SERVING

Calories: 300 Fat: 17g Carbs: 24.7g Protein: 17.2g

CREAMY MEXICAN STYLE CHICKEN

PREPARATION TIME
5'

COOK TIME
6 H

SERVING
6

INGREDIENTS

- 2 lb. chicken breasts
- 2 tbsp. Cumin
- 2 tbsp. Chili powder
- ½ tsp. Cayenne pepper
- ½ tsp. Black pepper
- ½ tsp. Sea salt
- 2 tbsp. Garlic powder
- 2 tbsp. Celery salt
- 2 tbsp. Onion powder
- ½ cup chicken stock

- 1 can (14 oz.) diced tomatoes & green chilies
- 1 cup sour cream
- 1 batch homemade taco seasoning

DIRECTIONS

1. Combine the spices.
2. Program the slow cooker using the low setting. Add all the fixings, adding the chicken last—cook for six hours on low.

NUTRIENTS PER SERVING

Calories: 262 Fat: 13g Carbs: 13g Protein: 32g

DELICIOUS RANCH CHICKEN

PREPARATION TIME
5'

COOK TIME
5 H

SERVING
6

INGREDIENTS

- 2 tsp. dried chives
- 1 ½ tsp. dried dill
- 1 tbsp. dried parsley
- Black pepper

½ t. each:
- Sea salt
- Garlic powder
- Paprika
- Onion
- 1 tbsp.ranch seasoning mix

- 3 skinless boneless chicken breasts
- 1 ½ tsp. steak seasoning basic rub mixture
- 3 shallots
- 12 bacon slices
- 6 cup broccoli florets
- 3 tbsp. red wine vinegar
- ½ cup mayonnaise

DIRECTIONS

1. Peel and slice the shallots and prepare the broccoli.
2. Prepare the chicken. Drizzle with the ranch and steak seasonings. Toss in the shallots. Place the top on the cooker for three to four hours on the low setting. Fold in the broccoli and continue cooking for another 30-45 minutes.
3. Transfer the chicken to a platter and shred using two forks. Add it back into the cooker with the juices. Stir in the vinegar and mayonnaise.

NUTRIENTS PER SERVING

Calories: 424 Fat: 23.3g Carbs: 4.75g Protein: 39g

MEDITERRANEAN CHICKEN

PREPARATION TIME
5'

COOK TIME
4 H

SERVING
3

INGREDIENTS

- 1 lb. chicken thighs
- 1 ½ tsp. olive oil (EVO)
- ½ cup roasted red peppers
- ½ thinly sliced sweet onion
- 1 ½ minced garlic cloves
- ¼ cup chicken broth
- ½ cup - any kind of olives

½ t. each:
- Rosemary
- Oregano

- Dried thyme
- ½ bay leaf
- ½ lemon

Optional:
- 1 ½ t. capers

DIRECTIONS

1. Pour the oil into a saucepan using the med-high heat setting. Brown the chicken. Cook the onions and garlic in the same skillet for four minutes.
2. Add the mixture to the slow cooker with the rest of the fixings (and chicken). Set the cooker on the low setting for four hours.

NUTRIENTS PER SERVING

Calories: 264 Fat: 11g Carbs: 8g Protein: 30g

CHICKEN CASSEROLE

PREPARATION TIME
5'

COOK TIME
3H

SERVING
3

INGREDIENTS

- 2 cubed boneless chicken breasts
- 1 can (8 oz.) tomato sauce
- Dash of pepper
- 1 tsp. Italian seasoning
- 1 bay leaf
- ¼ t. salt

For the Garnish:
- ½ cup shredded mozzarella cheese

DIRECTIONS

1. Chop the chicken into cubes.
2. Pour in the sauce and spices. Stir and cook on the low setting for three hours.

NUTRIENTS PER SERVING

Calories: 228 Fat: 8.8g Protein: 31.2g Carbs 6g

4-INGREDIENT JERK CHICKEN

PREPARATION TIME
5'

COOK TIME
5 H

SERVING
4

INGREDIENTS

- 5 chicken breasts
- 6 tsp. salt free Jerk seasoning spice
- 5 tsp. virgin olive oil
- 4 tsp. salt

DIRECTIONS

1. Rinse your chicken.
2. Mix with oil.
3. Rub Jerk seasoning and salt all over the chicken.
4. Cook on low for 5-6 hours.

NUTRIENTS PER SERVING

Calories: 200 Fat: 12g Protein: 31g Carbs: 9g

CHICKEN FAJITA SALAD

PREPARATION TIME	COOK TIME	SERVING
5'	4 H	4

INGREDIENTS

- 2 ½ lb. skinless boneless chicken breasts
- One 14.5 ounce can of diced tomatoes
- 2 cups yellow bell peppers
- 1 onion
- 4 minced garlic cloves
- ½ tsp. cumin
- ½ tsp. onion powder
- ½ tsp. chili powder
- Plenty of lettuce

DIRECTIONS

1. Put the chicken in the slow cooker and layer on onion and peppers.
2. Add everything else, with the diced tomatoes with their liquid poured in last.
3. Cook on high for 4 hours.

NUTRIENTS PER SERVING

Calories: 339 Fat: 8g Carbs: 9g Protein: 64g

CREAMY CHICKEN THIGHS

PREPARATION TIME
15'

COOK TIME
6 H

SERVING
4

INGREDIENTS

- 1lb. chicken thighs, skinless
- ¼ cup almond milk, unsweetened
- 1 tbsp. full-fat cream cheese
- 1 tsp. salt
- 1 onion, diced
- 1 tsp. paprika

DIRECTIONS

1. Mix the almond milk and full-fat cream.
2. Add salt, diced onion, and paprika.
3. Stir well.
4. Place the chicken thighs in the slow cooker.
5. Add the almond milk mixture and stir it.
6. Cook the chicken thighs for 6 hours on High.
7.

NUTRIENTS PER SERVING

Calories: 224 Fat: 14.3g Carbs: 4.7g Protein: 18.9g

JERK CHICKEN

PREPARATION TIME
25'

COOK TIME
5 H

SERVING
4

INGREDIENTS

- 1 tsp. nutmeg
- 1 tsp. cinnamon
- 1 tsp. minced garlic
- ½ tsp. cloves
- 1 tsp. ground coriander
- 1 tbsp. Erythritol
- 1lb. chicken thighs
- ½ cup water
- 1 tbsp. butter

DIRECTIONS

1. Mix the nutmeg, cinnamon, minced garlic, cloves, and ground coriander.
2. Add Erythritol and stir the ingredients.
3. Sprinkle the chicken thighs with the spice mixture.
4. Let the chicken thighs sit for 10 minutes to marinate, then put the chicken thighs in the slow cooker.
5. Add the butter and water.
6. Cook Jerk chicken for 5 hours on Low.

NUTRIENTS PER SERVING

Calories: 247 Fat: 11.5g Carbs: 4.9g Protein 33g

CHAPTER 10.
PORK

PULLED PORK

PREPARATION TIME
5'

COOK TIME
8 H

SERVING
8

INGREDIENTS

- 3 lb. pasture-raised pork shoulder.
- 2 tsp. onion powder
- 2 tsp. garlic powder
- 2 tsp. salt
- 2 tsp. paprika
- 1 tbsp. parsley
- 2 tsp. cumin
- ½ cup beer

DIRECTIONS

1. Place pork in a 6-quart slow cooker.
2. Stir together the remaining ingredients except for beer, and then rub this mixture all over the pork until evenly coated.
3. Pour in beer and cook for 8 hours at low heating setting.

NUTRIENTS PER SERVING

Calories 233: Fat 12g Protein: 20g Carbs: 2g

PORK ROAST

PREPARATION TIME
5'

COOK TIME
8 H

SERVING
6

INGREDIENTS

- 30 oz. pasture-raised pork shoulder
- 1 tsp. minced garlic
- ½ tsp. grated ginger
- ½ tbsp. salt
- ½ tsp. ground black pepper
- 2 tsp. dried thyme
- 1 tbsp. paprika powder
- 5 black peppercorns
- 1 bay leaf
- 1 tbsp. avocado oil

DIRECTIONS

1. Place pork in slow cooker, season with salt and thyme, add peppercorns and bay leaf, and then pour in water.
2. Cook for 8 hours at low heat setting.
3. Transfer pork to a baking dish.
4. Set oven to 450 degrees F and let preheat.
5. Stir together remaining ingredients, then brush mixture all over pork.
6. Place the baking sheet into the oven to bake pork for 10 minutes.

NUTRIENTS PER SERVING

Calories: 579 Fat: 11.6g Carbs: 4g Protein: 28g

PORK CHOPS

PREPARATION TIME
5'

COOK TIME
6 H

SERVING
6

INGREDIENTS

- 2 lb. pasture-raised pork chops
- 1 tsp. salt
- 1 tbsp. dried thyme
- 1 tbsp. dried rosemary
- 1 tbsp. ground cumin
- 1 tbsp. dried curry powder
- 1 tbsp. chopped fresh chives
- 1 tbsp. fennel seeds
- 4 tbsp. avocado oil

DIRECTIONS

1. Place 2 tbsp. oil in a small bowl, add remaining ingredients except for pork, and stir.
2. Rub this mixture on all sides of pork chops.
3. Grease slow cooker oil, add seasoned pork chops.
4. Cook pork for 6 hours at low heat setting.

NUTRIENTS PER SERVING

Calories: 235 Fat: 12g Carbs: 1g Protein 24g

SPICY PORK & SPINACH STEW

PREPARATION TIME
5'

COOK TIME
4 H

SERVING
5

INGREDIENTS

- 1lb. pasture-raised pork butt
- 6 cups baby spinach
- 10 oz. Rotel tomatoes
- 1 large white onion
- 4 cloves of garlic
- 1 tsp. dried thyme
- 2 tsp. Cajun seasoning blend
- 4 tbsp. avocado oil
- ¾ cup heavy whipping cream

DIRECTIONS

1. Place tomatoes, onion, and garlic in a food processor and pulse for 1 to 2 minutes.
2. Pour this mixture in a slow cooker, add Cajun seasoning mix, thyme, avocado oil, and pork pieces, and stir.
3. Cook for 5 hours at low heat setting.
4. Stir in cream until combined, add spinach and continue cooking at low heat setting for 20 minutes.

NUTRIENTS PER SERVING

Calories: 604 Fat: 12.7g Carbs: 3.3 g Protein: 56g

STUFFED TACO PEPPERS

PREPARATION TIME
5'

COOK TIME
8 H

SERVING
6

INGREDIENTS

- 1 cup cauliflower rice
- 6 small red bell peppers
- 18 oz. minced pork
- 1 tsp. garlic powder
- ¾ tsp. salt
- 1 tsp. red chili powder
- 1 cup shredded Monterey jack cheese
- 2 tbsp. avocado oil

DIRECTIONS

1. Place meat in a large bowl, add garlic, salt, and red chili powder, and stir.
2. Then stir in cauliflower rice and oil until combine, and then stir in cheese.
3. Stuff this mixture into each pepper and place them in a slow cooker.
4. Pour water.
5. Cook peppers for 4 hours at high heat setting and top peppers with more cheese in the last 10 minutes.

NUTRIENTS PER SERVING

Calories: 270 Fat: 22g Carbs: 4g Protein: 21g

CHINESE PULLED PORK

PREPARATION TIME
5'

COOK TIME
7 1/2 H

SERVING
6

INGREDIENTS

- 2.2 lb. pasture-raised pork shoulder
- 2 tbsp. garlic paste
- 2 tsp. ginger paste
- 1 tsp. smoked paprika
- 5 drops Erythritol sweetener
- 4 tbsp. soy sauce
- 1 tbsp. tomato paste
- 4 tbsp. tomato sauce
- 1 cup chicken broth

DIRECTIONS

1. Place pork in a slow cooker.
2. Whisk together the remaining ingredients until smooth, and then pour over the pork.
3. Cook for 7 hours at low heat setting.
4. Then shred pork with two forks and stir well until evenly coated with sauce.
5. Cook pork for 30 minutes.

NUTRIENTS PER SERVING

Calories: 447 Fat: 12g Carbs: 2g Protein: 30g

PULLED PORK WITH CARAMELIZED ONIONS

PREPARATION TIME
5'

COOK TIME
10 H

SERVING
8

INGREDIENTS

- 1 tbsp. olive oil
- 3 onions, sliced
- 1 cup raw cane sugar
- 1 tsp. dried oregano
- 4 garlic cloves
- 1/2 tsp. salt
- 1 tsp. pepper
- 1/2 cup cider vinegar
- 3 tsp. chipotle chili in adobo sauce
- 1 cup chili sauce

- 3 lb. pork shoulder

DIRECTIONS

1. Pour the oil in a pan over medium heat.
2. Sauté the onion for 3 to 6 minutes.
3. Add the sugar and continue cooking for 7 minutes more.
4. Stir in the oregano, garlic, salt, and pepper.
5. Cook for 1 minute.
6. Add the vinegar into the pan.
7. Bring to a boil, then simmer until the liquid has almost evaporated.
8. Remove the pan from the stove.
9. Mix in the chipotle and chili sauce.
10. Put the pork in a slow cooker.
11. Add the sauce from the pan.
12. Cook on low for 8 hours.
13. Remove the pork from the pot and shred the meat using 2 forks.
14. Place shredded meat back into the sauce.

NUTRIENTS PER SERVING

Calories: 355 Fat: 18g Carbs: 20g Protein: 25g

BACON WRAPPED PORK LOIN

PREPARATION TIME
5'

COOK TIME
7 H

SERVING
4

INGREDIENTS

- 2lb. pasture-raised pork loin roast, fat-trimmed
- 4 strips of bacon, uncooked
- 3 tbsp. dried onion soup mix, organic
- 1/4 cup water

DIRECTIONS

1. Pour water into a 6-quart slow cooker.
2. Rub seasoning mix on all sides of pork, then wrap with bacon and place into the slow cooker.
3. Plug in the slow cooker, then shut with lid and cook for 7 hours at low heat setting or 5 hours at high heat setting.
4. Serve straight away.

NUTRIENTS PER SERVING

Calories: 639 Fat: 4.2g Carbs: 0g Protein: 69g

MEATBALLS STUFFED WITH CHEESE

PREPARATION TIME
5'

COOK TIME
3 HOURS ON HIGH / 6
HOURS ON LOW

SERVING
4

INGREDIENTS

- 2 1/2 lb. ground pork, pasture-raised
- 1/2 cup pork rinds, crushed
- 1/2 tsp. garlic powder
- 1/2 tsp. salt
- 1/2 tsp. ground black pepper
- 2 tbsp. Italian seasonings
- 2 cup marinara sauce, sugar-free and organic
- 2 eggs
- 1/2 cup grated Parmesan cheese
- 8 oz. block of mozzarella cheese, cut into 24 pieces

DIRECTIONS

1. Crack eggs in a large bowl, add pork rind, garlic powder, salt, black pepper, and Italian seasoning, and whisk until combined.
2. Add ground meat, then mix until combined and shape the mixture into 24 meatballs.
3. Place a piece of cheese into the center of each meatball and then wrap the meat around it.
4. Pour half of the marinara sauce into the bottom of a 6-quart slow cooker, then arrange meatballs and cover with remaining sauce.
5. Plug in the slow cooker, shut with lid, and cook meatballs for 6 hours at low heat setting or 3 hours at high heat setting.
6. Serve straight away.

NUTRIENTS PER SERVING

Calories: 548 Fat: 12g Carbs: 6.5g Protein: 49g.

KALUA PIG

PREPARATION TIME
5'

COOK TIME
16 H

SERVING
8

INGREDIENTS

- 5 lb. pasture-raised pork shoulder, bone-in, and fat-trimmed
- 3 slices bacon
- 5 cloves garlic, peeled
- 2 tbsp. sea salt

DIRECTIONS

1. Make some cuts into the pork, then tuck garlic in them and season with salt.
2. Line a 6-quarts slow cooker with bacon slices, then top with seasoned pork and shut with lid.
3. Plug in the slow cooker and cook for 16 hours at low heat setting until very tender.
4. When done, transfer pork to a cutting board and shred pork with two forks.
5. Then taste pork to adjust seasoning and add cooking liquid to adjust seasoning.
6. Serve straightaway.

NUTRIENTS PER SERVING

Calories: 349 Fat: 27g Carbs: 0g Protein: 26.6g

CABBAGE ROLL SOUP

PREPARATION TIME
5'

COOK TIME
6 H

SERVING
4

INGREDIENTS

- 1lb. ground pork, pasture-raised
- 1 cup cauliflower rice
- 4 cups sliced cabbage
- ¼ cup chopped white onion
- ¼ cup chopped shallots
- ½ tsp. minced garlic
- ½ tsp. salt
- ½ tsp. ground black pepper
- ½ tsp. dried parsley
- ¼ tsp. dried oregano
- 1tbsp. avocado oil
- 8oz. marinara sauce, sugar-free
- 3 cups beef broth

DIRECTIONS

1. Place a medium skillet pan over medium-high heat, add oil and when hot, add onion and shallots and cook for 5 minutes or until softened.
2. Add garlic, cook for 30 seconds or until fragrant, then add pork and cook for 5 to 7 minutes or until nicely browned.
3. Season with salt, black pepper, parsley, and oregano, pour in marinara sauce, and stir well.
4. Then add cauliflower rice, stir until evenly coated, and transfer the mixture into a 6-quart slow cooker.
5. Plug in the slow cooker, pour in beef broth, then add cabbage and stir until combined.
6. Shut with lid and cook for 6 hours at low heat setting or 3 hours at high setting.
7. Serve straight away.

NUTRIENTS PER SERVING

Calories: 346 Fat: 26g Carbs: 6g Protein: 20g

PORK LOIN WITH PEANUT SAUCE

PREPARATION TIME
5'

COOK TIME
8 H

SERVING
4

INGREDIENTS

- 1lb. pork tenderloin
- 1tbsp. olive oil
- ½ tsp. salt
- ½ tsp. black pepper
- 1 cups cabbage, shredded
- ½ cup chicken stock
- ¼ cup peanut butter
- ¼ cup soy sauce
- ½ tbsp. rice vinegar
- ½ tbsp. crushed red pepper flakes

- ½ tbsp. cayenne pepper sauce
- 1 cloves garlic crushed and minced
- ¼ cup peanuts, chopped
- ½ tbsp. fresh lemongrass, chopped

DIRECTIONS

1. Brush the tenderloin with olive oil and season it with salt and black pepper.
2. Arrange the tenderloin and cabbage in a slow cooker.
3. In a bowl, combine the chicken stock, peanut butter, soy sauce, rice vinegar, crushed red pepper flakes, cayenne pepper sauce, and garlic. Whisk them together and pour the sauce into the slow cooker. Stir gently to distribute the sauce.
4. Sprinkle in the peanuts and lemongrass.
5. Cover and cook on low for 8 hours.

NUTRIENTS PER SERVING

Calories: 427 Fat: 25.5g Carbs: 6.9g Protein 20g

MACADAMIA CRUSTED PORK STEAKS

PREPARATION TIME
5'

COOK TIME
5 H

SERVING
4

INGREDIENTS

- 1lb. boneless pork steaks
- 1 tsp. allspice
- ½ tsp. nutmeg
- ½ tsp. ground ginger
- ½ tsp. cayenne powder
- ½ tsp. thyme
- ¼ cup buttermilk
- ½ cup macadamia nuts, chopped
- ¼ cup unsweetened shredded coconut
- 2 tbsp. coconut oil
- 1 tbsp. jalapeño pepper, diced
- ½ cup chicken stock
- 1 tbsp. lime juice
- 6 cups fresh spinach

DIRECTIONS

1. In a bowl, combine the allspice, nutmeg, ginger, cayenne powder, thyme, and buttermilk. Whisk together well.
2. Place the pork chops in the bowl and cover them with the buttermilk mixture. Allow them to saturate for 15 minutes.
3. In another bowl, combine the macadamia nuts and coconut.
4. Remove each pork chop and coat it on both sides with the crushed macadamia nuts and coconut.
5. Heat the coconut oil in a skillet over medium heat.
6. Add the pork chops and brown for approximately 2 minutes per side.
7. Place the spinach, jalapeño pepper, chicken stock, and lime juice in the slow cooker and stir gently to mix.
8. Add the pork steaks, cover, and cook on low for 5 ½ hours.

NUTRIENTS PER SERVING

Calories: 362 Fat: 27.4g Carbs: 5.8g Protein: 24.5g

SPARE RIBS

PREPARATION TIME	COOK TIME	SERVING
10'	8 H	6

INGREDIENTS

- 1lb. pork loin ribs
- 1 tsp. olive oil
- 1 tsp. minced garlic
- ¼ tsp. cumin
- ¼ tsp. chili powder
- 1 tbsp. butter
- 5 tbsp. water

DIRECTIONS

1. Mix the olive oil, minced garlic, cumin, and chili flakes in a bowl.
2. Melt the butter and add to the spice mixture.
3. Add water.
4. Rub the pork ribs with the spice mixture generously.
5. Cook the ribs for 8 hours on Low.

NUTRIENTS PER SERVING

Calories: 203 Fat: 14g Carbs: 10g Protein: 9.8g

PORK SHOULDER

PREPARATION TIME
25'

COOK TIME
7 H

SERVING
6

INGREDIENTS

- 1lb. pork shoulder
- 2 cups water
- 1 onion, peeled
- 2 garlic cloves, peeled
- 1 tsp. peppercorns
- 1 tsp. chili flakes
- ½ tsp. paprika
- 1 tsp. turmeric
- 1 tsp. cumin

DIRECTIONS

1. Sprinkle the pork shoulder with the peppercorns, chili flakes, paprika, turmeric, and cumin.
2. Stir it well, let it sit for 15 minutes to marinate.
3. Transfer the pork to the slow cooker.
4. Add water and peeled the onion.
5. Cook the pork shoulder for 7 hours on Low.

NUTRIENTS PER SERVING

Calories: 234 Fat: 16.4g Carbs: 2.8g Protein: 18g

CHAPTER 11.
LAMB

LAMB IN CURRY SAUCE

PREPARATION TIME
15'

COOK TIME
5 H

SERVING
4

INGREDIENTS

- 1 tsp. curry paste
- 1lb. lamb fillet, sliced
- 1 tbsp. pomegranate juice
- ½ cup water
- ½ cup coconut milk
- 1 onion, sliced
- 1 tsp. lemongrass
- 1 tbsp. coconut oil

DIRECTIONS

1. Melt the coconut oil in the skillet.
2. Add lamb fillet and roast it for 2 minutes per side on low heat.
3. After this, transfer the lamb in the slow cooker.
4. In the bowl, mix curry paste, pomegranate juice, coconut milk, water, and lemongrass.
5. Pour the liquid over the lamb.
6. Add sliced onion and cook the meal on High for 5 hours.

NUTRIENTS PER SERVING

Calories: 330 Fat: 19.6g Carbs: 4.7g Protein: 33g

ROSEMARY LAMB SHOULDER

PREPARATION TIME
30'

COOK TIME
9 H

SERVING
3

INGREDIENTS

- 9 oz. lamb shoulder
- 1 tbsp. fresh rosemary
- ½ cup apple cider vinegar
- 1 tbsp. olive oil
- 1 cup water
- 1 tsp. ground black pepper
- 2 garlic cloves, peeled

DIRECTIONS

1. Rub the lamb shoulder with olive oil and fresh rosemary.
2. Then put the lamb shoulder in the apple cider vinegar and leave for 30 minutes to marinate.
3. After this, transfer the lamb shoulder in the slow cooker.
4. Add water, ground black pepper, and garlic cloves.
5. Close the lid and cook the meat on low for 9 hours.

NUTRIENTS PER SERVING

Calories: 215 Fat: 11g Carbs: 2.2g Protein: 24g

LAMB SAUTE'

PREPARATION TIME
15'

COOK TIME
4 H

SERVING
5

INGREDIENTS

- 1 cup tomatoes, chopped
- 1 cup bell pepper, chopped
- 1 chili pepper, chopped
- 1 tbsp. avocado oil
- 12 oz. lamb fillet, chopped
- ½ cup criminal mushrooms, sliced
- 1 cup water

DIRECTIONS

1. Heat the avocado oil in the skillet well.
2. Add chopped lamb and roast it for 5 minutes. Stir the meat from time to time.
3. After this, transfer the meat in the slow cooker and add all remaining ingredients.
4. Close the lid and cook the sauté on High for 4.5 hours.

NUTRIENTS PER SERVING

Calories: 147g Fat: 5.5g Carbs: 3.7g Protein: 20g

AROMATIC LAMB

PREPARATION TIME	COOK TIME	SERVING
10'	4 H	2

INGREDIENTS

- 1 tbsp. minced garlic
- 1 tsp. ground black pepper
- ½ tsp. salt
- 1 tsp. sesame oil
- 1lb. lamb sirloin, chopped
- ½ cup water

DIRECTIONS

1. Mix the lamb with minced garlic, ground black pepper, and salt.
2. Then sprinkle the meat with sesame oil and transfer in the slow cooker.
3. Add water and cook the meat on low for 8 hours.

NUTRIENTS PER SERVING

Calories: 246 Fat: 11.6g Protein: 32.3 g Carbs: 1g

SWEET LAMB TAGINE

PREPARATION TIME
10'

COOK TIME
10 H

SERVING
6

INGREDIENTS

- 12 oz. lamb fillet, chopped
- 1 cup apricots, pitted, chopped
- 1 cup red wine
- 1 jalapeno pepper, sliced
- 1 tsp. ground nutmeg
- 1 cup water
- 1 tsp. ground ginger

DIRECTIONS

1. Mix lamb with ground nutmeg and ground ginger.
2. Transfer the lamb meat in the slow cooker.
3. Add water, jalapeno pepper, red wine, and apricots.
4. Close the lid and cook the tagine for 10 hours on Low.

NUTRIENTS PER SERVING

Calories: 154 Fat: 4.5g Carbs: 4.4g Protein: 16.4g

LAMB MEATBALLS

PREPARATION TIME
10'

COOK TIME
4 H

SERVING
8 MEATBALLS (SERVING
SIZE = 2 MEATBALLS)

INGREDIENTS

- 4tbsp. minced onion
- 18 oz. lamb fillet, minced
- 2tsp. Italian seasonings
- 2tsp. flour
- 2tbsp. olive oil
- 1tsp. salt
- 1 cup water

DIRECTIONS

1. In the bowl, mix minced lamb, minced onion, Italian seasonings, flour, and salt.
2. Make the small meatballs.
3. After this, preheat the olive oil in the skillet.
4. Add meatballs and roast them on high heat for 30 seconds per side.
5. Then transfer the meatballs in the slow cooker.
6. Add water and cook the meal on high for 4 hours.

NUTRIENTS PER SERVING 2 MEATBALLS

Calories: 314 Fat: 17g Carbs: 2g Protein: 36g

HOT LAMB STRIPS

PREPARATION TIME
7'

COOK TIME
5 H

SERVING
6

INGREDIENTS

- 14 oz. lamb fillet, cut into strips
- 1 tsp. cayenne pepper
- 2 tbsp. butter, melted
- 1 tbsp. hot sauce
- ½ cup water

DIRECTIONS

1. Mix lamb strips with hot sauce and cayenne pepper.
2. Transfer them in the slow cooker.
3. After this, add water and butter.
4. Close the lid and cook the lamb on High for 5 hours.

NUTRIENTS PER SERVING

Calories: 158 Fat: 8.8g Carbs: 0.2g Protein: 18.7g

BRAISED LAMB SHANK

PREPARATION TIME
10'

COOK TIME
10 H

SERVING
4

INGREDIENTS

- 4 lamb shanks
- 1 cup water
- ½ cup tomato juice
- 1 tbsp. corn flour
- 1 tsp. salt
- 1 tsp. cayenne pepper
- 1 onion, chopped
- ½ carrot, chopped

DIRECTIONS

1. Mix tomato juice with corn flour and pour the liquid in the slow cooker.
2. Add lamb shanks, water, salt, cayenne pepper, onion, and carrot.
3. Close the lid and cook the meat on low for 10 hours.

NUTRIENTS PER SERVING

Calories: 427 Fat: 19.2g Carbs: 25.3g Protein: 33.8g

SWEET LAMB RIBS

PREPARATION TIME
10'

COOK TIME
9 H

SERVING
3

INGREDIENTS

- 8 oz. lamb ribs, chopped
- 1 tsp. tomato paste
- 2 tsp. liquid honey
- ½ cup butter
- ¼ cup water

DIRECTIONS

1. Rub the lamb ribs with tomato paste and liquid honey.
2. Then place them in the slow cooker.
3. Add butter and water.
4. Close the lid and cook the meat on low for 9 hours.

NUTRIENTS PER SERVING

Calories: 414g Fat: 37.4g Carbs: 4.2g Protein: 15.8g

EASY LAMB CHOPS

PREPARATION TIME	COOK TIME	SERVING
10'	5 H	4

INGREDIENTS

- 4 lamb chops
- ½ tsp. salt
- 1 tsp. sesame oil
- 1/3 cup water

DIRECTIONS

1. Sprinkle the lamb chops with sesame oil, salt, and ground black pepper.
2. Place the lamb chops in the slow cooker and add water.
3. Close the lid and cook the meal on High for 5 hours.

NUTRIENTS PER SERVING

Calories: 169 Fat: 7.4g Carbs: 0.3g Protein: 24g

LAMB WITH CAPERS

PREPARATION TIME
5'

COOK TIME
4 H

SERVING
2

INGREDIENTS

- 1lb. lamb chops
- 1 tbsp. capers
- ½ cup beef stock
- ¼ cup tomato passata
- ½ tsp. sweet paprika
- ½ tsp. chili powder
- 2 tbsp. olive oil
- 3 scallions, chopped
- A pinch of salt and black pepper

DIRECTIONS

1. In your Slow Cooker, mix the lamb chops with the capers, stock, and the other ingredients, toss, put the lid on and cook on High for 4 hours. Divide the mix between plates and serve.

NUTRIENTS PER SERVING

Calories: 244 Fat: 12g Carbs: 5g Protein: 16g

LAMB AND CABBAGE

PREPARATION TIME
5'

COOK TIME
5 H

SERVING
2

INGREDIENTS

- 2 lb. lamb stew meat, cubed
- 1 cup red cabbage, shredded
- 1 cup beef stock
- 1 tsp. avocado oil
- 1 tsp. sweet paprika
- 2 tbsp. tomato paste
- A pinch of salt and black pepper
- 1 tbsp. cilantro, chopped

DIRECTIONS

1. In your Slow Cooker, mix the lamb with the cabbage, stock, and the other ingredients, toss, put the lid on and cook on High for 5 hours. Divide everything between plates and serve.

NUTRIENTS PER SERVING

Calories: 254 Fat: 12g Carbs: 6g Protein: 16g

LAMB CHOPS WITH TOMATO PUREE

PREPARATION TIME
15'

COOK TIME
3 H

SERVING
2

INGREDIENTS

- 10 oz. lamb chops
- 1 tbsp. tomato puree
- ½ tsp. cumin
- ½ tsp. ground coriander
- 1 tsp. garlic powder
- 1 tsp. butter
- 5 tbsp. water

DIRECTIONS

1. Mix the tomato puree, cumin, ground coriander, garlic powder, and water.
2. Brush the lamb chops with the tomato puree mixture on each side and let marinate for 20 minutes.
3. Toss the butter in the slow cooker.
4. Add the lamb chops.
5. Cook the lamb chops for 3 hours on High.

NUTRIENTS PER SERVING

Calories: 290 Fat: 12.5g Carbs: 2g Protein: 40.3g

ROSEMARY LEG OF LAMB

PREPARATION TIME
15'

COOK TIME
7 H

SERVING
8

INGREDIENTS

- 2 lb. leg of lamb
- 1 onion
- 3 cups water
- 1 garlic clove, peeled
- 1 tbsp. mustard seeds
- 1 tsp. salt
- ½ tsp. turmeric
- 1 tsp. ground black pepper

DIRECTIONS

1. Chop the garlic clove and combine it with the mustard seeds, turmeric, black pepper, and salt.
2. Peel the onion and grate it.
3. Mix the grated onion and spice mixture.
4. Rub the leg of lamb with the grated onion mixture.
5. Put the leg of lamb in the slow cooker and cook it for 7 hours on Low.

NUTRIENTS PER SERVING

Calories: 225 Fat: 8.7g Carbs: 2.2g Protein: 32.4g

CHAPTER 12.
BEEF

MEAT PIE

PREPARATION TIME
5'

COOK TIME
6 H

SERVING
6

INGREDIENTS

- 1 ½ lb. ground beef
- 1 egg
- ½ cup almonds ground finely into a flour
- ½ cup Parmesan cheese, freshly grated
- ½ cup green bell pepper, diced
- ½ cup onion, diced
- 1 tsp. salt
- 1 tsp. black pepper
- 1 tbsp. fresh oregano
- 2 cups tomatoes, chopped
- 2 cloves garlic, crushed and minced
- ½ cup fresh basil, chopped
- 1 cup fresh mozzarella, sliced

DIRECTIONS

1. In a bowl, combine the ground beef, egg, almonds, Parmesan cheese, green bell pepper, and onion.
2. Season the mixture with salt, black pepper, and oregano. Mix well.
3. Line a slow cooker with aluminum foil for easier removal, if desired.
4. Take the meat mixture and press it firmly into the bottom of the slow cooker.
5. Place the tomatoes, garlic, and basil in a blender and puree.
6. Pour the tomato mixture over the meat.
7. Cover and cook on low for 6 hours.
8. Remove the lid and arrange the mozzarella cheese slices over the top. Replace the cover and cook for an additional 30 minutes before serving.

NUTRIENTS PER SERVING

Calories: 407 Fat: 31.7g Carbs: 5g Protein: 23.7g

MEXICAN MEATLOAF

PREPARATION TIME
5'

COOK TIME
7 H

SERVING
6

INGREDIENTS

- 1 ½ lb. ground beef
- 1 egg
- 1 cup añejo cheese, grated
- 1 cup onion, diced
- 2 tbsp. jalapeño pepper, diced
- ¼ cup fresh cilantro, chopped
- 2 tsp. chili powder
- 1 tsp. ground cumin
- 1 tsp. salt
- 1 tsp. black pepper
- 1 cup roasted tomatoes, chopped
- ½ cup Mexican crema
- 1 avocado, sliced

DIRECTIONS

1. In a bowl, combine the ground beef, egg, añejo cheese, onion, and jalapeño pepper.
2. Season the mixture with the cilantro, chili powder, cumin, salt, and black pepper. Mix well.
3. Line a slow cooker with aluminum foil for easier removal, if desired.
4. Take the meat mixture and either form it into a loaf and place it in the slow cooker, or press the meat mixture into the bottom of the slow cooker.
5. Add the tomatoes on top of the meatloaf.
6. Cover and cook on low for 7 hours or until cooked through.
7. Serve garnished with a dollop of Mexican crema and sliced avocado.

NUTRIENTS PER SERVING

Calories: 545 Fat: 45.6g Carbs: 5g Protein: 26.7g

CORNED BEEF

PREPARATION TIME
10'

COOK TIME
8 H

SERVING
6

INGREDIENTS

- 1lb. corned beef
- 1 tsp. peppercorns
- 1 tsp. chili flakes
- 1 tsp. mustard seeds
- 1 bay leaf
- 1 tsp. salt
- 1 oz. bacon fat
- 4 garlic cloves
- 1 cup water
- 1 tbsp. butter

DIRECTIONS

1. Mix the peppercorns, chili flakes, mustard seeds, and salt.
2. Rub the corned beef with the spice mixture well.
3. Add the corned beef.
4. Add water, butter, and bay leaf.
5. Add the bacon fat.
6. Cook the corned beef for 8 hours on Low.

NUTRIENTS PER SERVING

Calories: 178 Fat: 13.5g Carbs: 1.3g Protein: 12.2g

WHISKEY BLUES STEAK

PREPARATION TIME
5'

COOK TIME
6 H

SERVING
6

INGREDIENTS

- 1 ½ lb. beef steak
- 1 tsp. salt
- 2 tsp. coarsely ground black pepper
- 3 cups zucchini, sliced thick
- ¼ cup butter
- 1 cup onions, sliced
- ¼ cup whiskey
- 2 cloves garlic, crushed and minced
- ½ cup blue cheese, crumbled

DIRECTIONS

1. Season the steak with salt and black pepper.
2. Place the sliced zucchini in the bottom of the slow cooker.
3. Melt the butter in a skillet over medium-high heat. Add the steaks to the skillet and brown on both sides, approximately 2-4 minutes.
4. Remove the steaks from the skillet and place them in the slow cooker.
5. Add the onions to the skillet and sauté until crisp tender, approximately 3-4 minutes.
6. Add the whiskey and cook until reduced, 1-2 minutes, scraping the bottom of the skillet.
7. Transfer the onions to the slow cooker and sprinkle in the garlic.
8. Cover and cook on low for 6 hours, or until the steaks are cooked to the desired doneness and are tender.
9. Serve the steaks garnished with blue cheese.

NUTRIENTS PER SERVING

Calories: 305 Fat: 15.4g Carbs: 6.g Protein: 29.2g

PHILLY CHEESE STEAK

PREPARATION TIME
15'

COOK TIME
3 H

SERVING
4

INGREDIENTS

- 1 ½ lb. beef steak, sliced thin
- 1 cup green bell pepper, sliced
- 1 cup onion, sliced
- ¼ cup butter melted
- 4 cloves garlic, crushed and minced
- ¼ cup Worcestershire sauce
- ¼ cup beef stock
- ¼ cup soy sauce
- 1 tsp. salt
- 1 tsp. black pepper
- 1 tsp. paprika
- 1 cup Swiss cheese, shredded
- Bibb lettuce leaves or approved keto bread for serving (optional)

DIRECTIONS

1. Place the green bell pepper and the onion in a slow cooker.
2. Pour in the butter and toss to coat.
3. Add the sliced beef steak into the slow cooker.
4. In a bowl, combine the garlic, Worcestershire sauce, beef stock, soy sauce, salt, black pepper, and paprika. Mix well and pour the liquid into the slow cooker.
5. Cover the slow cooker and cook on high for 4 hours.
6. Remove the lid and sprinkle in the Swiss cheese.
7. Replace the cover, turn the heat to low, and cook an additional 30 minutes before serving.

NUTRIENTS PER SERVING

Calories: 312.6 Fat: 17.1 g Carbs: 6.6g Protein: 32.2g

STEAK STUFFED PEPPERS

PREPARATION TIME	COOK TIME	SERVING
5'	4 H	4

INGREDIENTS

- 4 red bell peppers
- 2 tbsp. butter
- 1 lb. beef steak, sliced thin
- 1 tsp. salt
- 1 tsp. black pepper
- 1 tbsp. fresh rosemary, finely chopped
- ¼ cup fresh basil, chopped
- 4 cloves garlic, crushed and minced
- 1 cup tomatoes, chopped
- ½ cup onion, diced
- ½ cup celery, diced
- ½ cup walnuts, chopped
- ½ cup Stilton cheese, crumbled
- 1 cup beef stock or water

DIRECTIONS

1. Cut the tops off the bell peppers and scoop the seeds out.
2. Melt the butter in a skillet over medium heat.
3. Place the steak in the skillet and cook for 1-2 minutes.
4. Season the steak with salt, black pepper, rosemary, basil, and garlic.
5. Add the tomatoes and cook for an additional 2-3 minutes. Remove the steak from the heat and allow it to cool enough to handle.
6. Combine the steak with the onion, celery, walnuts, and Stilton cheese.
7. Scoop equal amounts of the steak mixture into each of the peppers.
8. Pour the beef stock or water into the slow cooker.
9. Replace the tops on the peppers and arrange them in the slow cooker.
10. Cover and cook on high for 4 hours.

NUTRIENTS PER SERVING

Calories: 397 Fat 26.4g Carbs: 11g Protein: 33g

BEST EASY BEEF CASSEROLE

PREPARATION TIME
5'

COOK TIME
6 H

SERVING
6

INGREDIENTS

- 1 ½ lb. ground beef
- 1 tsp. salt
- 1 tsp. black pepper
- 1 tsp. garlic powder
- 1 tsp. paprika
- 1 cup onion, chopped
- 4 cups frozen spinach
- 2 cups white mushrooms, quartered
- 1 cup tomatoes, chopped
- 1 cup cream cheese
- 1 cup white cheddar cheese, shredded

DIRECTIONS

1. Place the ground beef in a slow cooker and season with salt, black pepper, garlic powder, and paprika.
2. Add the onion, spinach, mushrooms, and tomatoes. Stir gently.
3. Cover and cook on low for 6 hours.
4. Combine the cream cheese and white cheddar cheese.
5. Add the cheese mixture to the slow cooker and stir gently.
6. Replace the cover on the slow cooker and cook for an additional 30-40 minutes before serving.

NUTRIENTS PER SERVING

Calories: 464.6 Fat: 35.7g Carbs: 13g Protein: 26.2g

SPICY CITRUS MEATBALLS

PREPARATION TIME
5'

COOK TIME
8 H

SERVING
6

INGREDIENTS

- 1 ½ lb. ground beef
- 1 egg
- 1 tbsp. Worcestershire sauce
- 1 tbsp. garlic chili sauce
- ½ cup onion, diced
- 1 cup zucchini, shredded
- 2 tbsp. olive oil
- 3 cups green beans, trimmed
- 1 cup beef stock
- 1 tbsp. crushed red pepper flakes
- ¼ cup soy sauce
- 1 tsp. orange extract
- 1 tsp. black pepper

DIRECTIONS

1. In a bowl, combine the ground beef, egg, Worcestershire sauce, garlic chili sauce, onion, and zucchini. Mix well.
2. Take the spoonful of the meat mixture and form them into golf ball sized meatballs.
3. Pour the olive oil into a skillet over medium heat.
4. Place the meatballs in the skillet and cook just until browned on all sides.
5. Place the green beans in the slow cooker.
6. Transfer the meatballs from the skillet to the slow cooker.
7. Combine the beef stock, crushed red pepper flakes, soy sauce, orange extract, and black pepper. Mix well and pour into the slow cooker.
8. Cover and cook on low for 8 hours.

NUTRIENTS PER SERVING

Calories: 435 Fat: 35.8g Carbs: 6.5g Protein 21.7g

BEEF IN SAUCE

PREPARATION TIME
10'

COOK TIME
9 H

SERVING
4

INGREDIENTS

- 1lb. beef stew meat, chopped
- 1 tsp. gram masala
- 1 cup water
- 1 tbsp. flour
- 1 tsp. garlic powder
- 1 onion, diced

DIRECTIONS

1. Whisk flour with water until smooth and pour the liquid in the slow cooker.
2. Add gram masala and beef stew meat.
3. After this, add onion and garlic powder.
4. Close the lid and cook the meat on low for 9 hours.
5. Serve the cooked beef with thick gravy from the slow cooker.

NUTRIENTS PER SERVING

Calories: 231 Fat 7g Carbs: 4.6g Protein: 35g

BEEF WITH GREENS

PREPARATION TIME
15'

COOK TIME
8 H

SERVING
3

INGREDIENTS

- 1 cup fresh spinach, chopped
- 9 oz. beef stew meat, cubed
- 1 cup Swiss chard, chopped
- 2 cups water
- 1 tsp. olive oil
- 1 tsp. dried rosemary

DIRECTIONS

1. Heat olive oil in the skillet.
2. Add beef and roast it for 1 minute per side.
3. Then transfer the meat in the slow cooker.
4. Add Swiss chard, spinach, water, and rosemary.
5. Close the lid and cook the meal on Low for 8 hours.

NUTRIENTS PER SERVING

Calories: 177 Fat: 7g Carbs: 1g Protein: 26.3g

SPICY BALSAMIC BEEF

PREPARATION TIME
15'

COOK TIME
9 H

SERVING
4

INGREDIENTS

- 1lb. beef stew meat, cubed
- 1 tsp. cayenne pepper
- 4 tbsp. balsamic vinegar
- ½ cup water
- 2 tbsp. butter

DIRECTIONS

1. Toss the butter in the skillet and melt it.
2. Then add meat and roast it for 2 minutes per side on medium heat.
3. Transfer the meat with butter in the slow cooker.
4. Add balsamic vinegar, cayenne pepper, and water.
5. Close the lid and cook the meal on Low for 9 hours.

NUTRIENTS PER SERVING

Calories: 266 Fat: 13g Carbs: 0.4g Protein: 34.5g

BALSAMIC BEEF

PREPARATION TIME
20'

COOK TIME
7 H

SERVING
4

INGREDIENTS

- 2 tbsp. balsamic vinegar
- 1 tbsp. olive oil
- 1 lb. beef loin
- 1 tsp. minced garlic
- ½ tsp. ground coriander
- 1 tsp. cumin
- ½ tsp. dried dill
- 2 tbsp. water

DIRECTIONS

1. Chop the beef loin roughly and place it in a large bowl, then sprinkle it with the balsamic vinegar.
2. Add olive oil, minced garlic, ground coriander, cumin, and dried dill.
3. Stir the meat well and let sit for 10 minutes.
4. Place the meat in the slow cooker and add water.
5. Cook the beef for 7 hours on Low.

NUTRIENTS PER SERVING

Calories: 241 Fat: 13g Carbs: 0.6g Protein: 30.5g

ONION BEEF

PREPARATION TIME
10'

COOK TIME
5 H

SERVING
14

INGREDIENTS

- 4lb. beef sirloin, sliced
- 2 cups white onion, chopped
- 3 cups water
- ½ cup butter
- 1 tsp. ground black pepper
- 1 tsp. salt
- 1 bay leaf

DIRECTIONS

1. Mix beef sirloin with salt and ground black pepper and transfer in the slow cooker.
2. Add butter, water, onion, and bay leaf.
3. Close the lid and cook the meat on High for 5.5 hours.

NUTRIENTS PER SERVING

Calories: 306 Fat: 14.7g Carbs: 1.7g Protein: 39.6g

PEPPERED STEAK

PREPARATION TIME
15'

COOK TIME
4 H

SERVING
4

INGREDIENTS

- 10 oz. Sirloin Steak
- 3 cups water
- 1 tbsp. peppercorns
- 1 tsp. salt
- ½ tsp. ground nutmeg
- 2 garlic cloves, peeled
- 1 tsp. olive oil

DIRECTIONS

1. Make the small cuts in the sirloin and chop the garlic cloves.
2. Place the garlic cloves in the sirloin cuts.
3. Sprinkle the steak with the salt, ground nutmeg, and peppercorns.
4. Transfer the steak in the slow cooker and add water.
5. Cook the steak for 4 hours on Low.
6. Then remove the steak from the slow cooker and slice it.

NUTRIENTS PER SERVING

Calories: 192 Fat: 12g Carbs: 1g Protein: 12g

CHAPTER 13.
SIDE DISHES

SUMMER VEGGIES SURPRISE

PREPARATION TIME
10'

COOK TIME
3 H

SERVING
4

INGREDIENTS

- 1 and ½ cups red onion, cut into medium chunks
- 1 cup cherry tomatoes, halved
- 2 cups okra, sliced
- 2 and ½ cups zucchini, sliced
- 2 cups yellow bell pepper, chopped
- 1 cup mushrooms, sliced
- 2 tbsp. basil, chopped
- 1 tbsp. thyme, chopped
- ½ cup olive oil
- ½ cup balsamic vinegar

DIRECTIONS

1. In a large bowl, mix onion chunks with tomatoes, okra, zucchini, bell pepper, mushrooms, basil, and thyme.
2. Add oil and vinegar and toss to coat everything.
3. Transfer to your slow cooker, cover, and cook on High for 3 hours.

NUTRIENTS PER SERVING

Calories: 150 Fat: 2g Carbs: 6g Protein: 5g

SIMPLE BROCCOLI MIX

PREPARATION TIME
10'

COOK TIME
2,30 H

SERVING
10

INGREDIENTS

- 10 oz. coconut cream
- 6 cups broccoli florets
- ¼ cup yellow onion, chopped
- A pinch of salt and black pepper

DIRECTIONS

1. In your slow cooker, combine the broccoli with the cream, onion, salt, and pepper, cover, and cook on High for 2 hours and 30 minutes.
2. Divide between plates and serve.

NUTRIENTS PER SERVING

Calories: 160 Fat: 6g Carbs: 11g Protein: 6g

DELICIOUS GREEN BEANS MIX

PREPARATION TIME
10'

COOK TIME
2 H

SERVING
12

INGREDIENTS

- 16 cups green beans
- ½ cup coconut sugar
- ½ cup olive oil
- 1 tsp. coconut amino
- 1 tsp. garlic powder

DIRECTIONS

1. Put the oil in your slow cooker, add green beans, sugar, amino, and garlic powder, toss, cover, and cook on Low for 2 hours.
2. Divide between plates and serve as a side dish.
3. Enjoy!

NUTRIENTS PER SERVING

Calories: 162 Fat: 7g Carbs: 12g Protein: 3g

MUSHROOM CAULIFLOWER RICE

PREPARATION TIME
10'

COOK TIME
3 H

SERVING
6

INGREDIENTS

- 1 cup cauliflower rice
- 6 green onions, chopped
- 2 tbsp. olive oil
- 2 garlic cloves, minced
- ½ lb. baby Portobello mushrooms, sliced
- 1 and ½ cups veggie stock

DIRECTIONS

1. In your slow cooker, combine the cauliflower rice with the green onions, oil, garlic, mushrooms, and veggie stock, cover, cook on Low for 3 hours, divide between plates and serve as a side dish.

NUTRIENTS PER SERVING

Calories: 172 Fat: 5g Carbs: 14g Protein: 6g

BUTTERNUT MIX

PREPARATION TIME
10'

COOK TIME
4 H

SERVING
8

INGREDIENTS

- 1 yellow onion, chopped
- 1 cup carrots, chopped
- 1 tbsp. olive oil
- 1 and ½ tsp. curry powder
- 1 garlic clove, minced
- ¼ tsp. ginger, grated
- ½ tsp. cinnamon powder
- 1 butternut squash, cubed
- 2 cups veggie stock
- ¾ cup coconut milk

DIRECTIONS

1. Heat up a pan with the oil over medium-high heat, add onion, carrots, and garlic, stir, cook for 4-5 minutes and transfer to your slow cooker.
2. Add curry powder, ginger, cinnamon, squash, and stock, cover, and cook on Low for 3 hours and 30 minutes.
3. Add milk, toss, cover, cook on Low for 30 minutes more, divide between plates, and serve.

NUTRIENTS PER SERVING

Calories: 212 Fat: 6g Carbs: 14g Protein: 4g

SAUSAGE SIDE DISH

PREPARATION TIME
10'

COOK TIME
2 H

SERVING
4

INGREDIENTS

- 1lb. pork sausage, minced
- ½ lb. mushrooms, chopped
- 2 tbsp. olive oil
- 2 yellow onion, chopped
- 2 garlic cloves, minced
- 6 celery ribs, chopped
- 1 cup chicken stock
- 1 tbsp. sage, chopped
- 1 cup cranberries
- ½ cup sunflower seeds

DIRECTIONS

1. Grease your slow cooker with the oil, add sausage, mushrooms, onion, garlic, celery, stock, sage, cranberries, and sunflower seeds.
2. Cover, cook on Low for 2 hours, divide between plates and serve as a side dish.

NUTRIENTS PER SERVING

Calories: 200 Fat: 4g Carbs: 14g Protein: 7g

PARSLEY SWEET POTATOES

PREPARATION TIME
10'

COOK TIME
6 H

SERVING
6

INGREDIENTS

- 1 and ½ lb. sweet potatoes, peeled and cubed
- 1 carrot, sliced
- 1 celery rib, chopped
- ¼ cup yellow onion, chopped
- 2 cups chicken stock
- 1 tbsp. parsley, chopped
- 1 garlic clove, minced
- A pinch of salt and black pepper

DIRECTIONS

1. In your slow cooker, combine the sweet potatoes with the carrot, celery, onion, stock, parsley, garlic, salt, and pepper.
2. Toss, cover, and cook on Low for 6 hours.

NUTRIENTS PER SERVING

Calories: 114 Fat: 4g Carbs: 15g Protein: 4g

SWEET CABBAGE

PREPARATION TIME	COOK TIME	SERVING
10'	6 H	4

INGREDIENTS

- 1 onion, sliced
- 1 cabbage, shredded
- 2 apples, peeled, cored and roughly chopped
- A pinch of sea salt
- Black pepper to the taste
- 1 cup apple juice
- ½ cup chicken stock
- 3 tbsp. mustard
- 1 tbsp. coconut oil

DIRECTIONS

1. Grease your slow cooker with the coconut oil and place apples, cabbage, and onions inside.
2. Mix stock with mustard, a pinch of salt, black pepper, and the apple juice and whisk.
3. Pour this over into the slow cooker as well, cover, and cook on Low for 6 hours.

NUTRIENTS PER SERVING

Calories: 200 Fat: 4g Carbs: 8g Protein: 6g

DELICIOUS SWEET POTATOES AND BACON

PREPARATION TIME
10'

COOK TIME
3 H

SERVING
4

INGREDIENTS

- ½ cup orange juice
- 4 lb. sweet potatoes, sliced
- 3 tbsp. agave nectar
- ½ tsp. thyme, dried
- ½ tsp. sage, crushed
- A pinch of sea salt
- 2 tbsp. olive oil
- 4 bacon slices, cooked and crumbled

DIRECTIONS

1. In your slow cooker, mix sweet potato slices with orange juice, agave nectar, thyme, sage, sea salt, olive oil, and bacon.
2. Cover and cook on High for 3 hours.

NUTRIENTS PER SERVING

Calories: 189 Fat: 4g Carbs: 9g Protein: 5g

FLAVORED CARROTS

PREPARATION TIME
10'

COOK TIME
6 H

SERVING
6

INGREDIENTS

- 2 lb. sweet carrots
- ½ cup peaches, chopped
- 2 tbsp. olive oil
- ¼ cup coconut sugar
- ½ tsp. cinnamon powder
- 1 tsp. vanilla extract
- A pinch of nutmeg, ground
- 2 tbsp. water

DIRECTIONS

1. In your slow cooker, combine the carrots with peaches, oil, sugar, cinnamon, vanilla, nutmeg, and water.
2. Ttoss, cover, cook on Low for 6 hours, divide between plates and serve.

NUTRIENTS PER SERVING

Calories: 190 Fat: 7g Carbs: 16g Protein: 3g

EASY BUTTERNUT SQUASH

PREPARATION TIME
10'

COOK TIME
4 H

SERVING
6

INGREDIENTS

- ½ butternut squash, cubed
- ½ yellow onion, chopped
- ¼ cup chicken stock
- 1tsp. thyme, chopped
- 2 garlic cloves, minced
- 3oz. baby spinach
- Salt and black pepper to taste

DIRECTIONS

1. In your slow cooker, combine the squash with the onion, stock, thyme, garlic, salt, and pepper
2. Toss, cover, and cook on Low for 4 hours.

NUTRIENTS PER SERVING

Calories: 100 Fat: 2g Carbs: 15g Protein: 5g

TASTY MUSHROOM MIX

PREPARATION TIME
10'

COOK TIME
4 H

SERVING
6

INGREDIENTS

- 1 lb. mushrooms, halved
- 2 tbsp. olive oil
- 1 yellow onion, sliced
- 1 tsp. Italian seasoning
- ¼ cup veggie stock

DIRECTIONS

1. In your slow cooker, combine the mushrooms with the oil, onion, Italian seasoning, and stock.
2. Toss, cover, and cook on Low for 4 hours.

NUTRIENTS PER SERVING

Calories: 120 Fat: 7g Carbs: 8g Protein: 5g

EASY KETO MEATBALLS

PREPARATION TIME
5'

COOK TIME
2 H

SERVING
6 (18 MEATBALLS—3
MEATBALLS EACH)

INGREDIENTS

- 2lb. grass-fed beef
- 2 cups beef stock
- 2tbsp. no-sugar tomato paste
- 1tbsp. cumin
- 1tsp. Italian seasoning
- 1tsp. paprika
- Salt and pepper to taste

DIRECTIONS

1. Mix meat with seasonings and form into balls.
2. Put in your slow cooker.
3. Mix stock and tomato paste until smooth.
4. Pour over meatballs.
5. Cook on high for 2 hours.

NUTRIENTS PER SERVING

Calories: 275 Fat: 15g Carbs: 1g Protein: 32g

SWEET'N SPICY SHRIMP

PREPARATION TIME	COOK TIME	SERVING
5'	40 MIN	6

INGREDIENTS

- 2 lb. peeled and cleaned raw shrimp
- ¾ cup extra virgin olive oil
- 4 tsp. liquid stevia
- 2 tsp. Sriracha sauce
- 1 tsp. sweet paprika
- Pinch of red pepper flakes
- Salt and pepper to taste

DIRECTIONS

1. Mix olive oil, stevia, Sriracha sauce, paprika, red pepper flakes, salt, and pepper in your slow cooker.
2. Cook on high for 30 minutes.
3. Add raw shrimp and stir to coat.
4. Cook on high for 10 minutes.

NUTRIENTS PER SERVING

Calories: 359 Fat: 30g Carbs: 2g Protein: 21g

CREAMY CHEESY BRUSSELS SPROUTS DIP

PREPARATION TIME
5'

COOK TIME
2 H

SERVING
6

INGREDIENTS

- 1 lb. trimmed and quartered Brussels sprouts
- 4 slices bacon
- ¾ cup shredded mozzarella cheese
- 4-oz. room temperature cream cheese
- ¼ cup sour cream
- ¼ cup mayo
- ¼ cup grated parmesan cheese
- 3 minced garlic cloves
- 1 tbsp. extra-virgin olive oil
- Salt and pepper to taste

DIRECTIONS

1. Mix Brussels sprouts in the oil, salt, and pepper.
2. Spread on a baking sheet with minced garlic
3. Put in a 400-degree oven for 20 minutes to roast, turning at the 10-minute mark.
4. Mix all the rest of the ingredients together (except bacon) and add roasted sprouts and garlic
5. Put in the slow cooker for 1 hour on high, and then check.
6. While that's cooking, cook your bacon in a skillet.
7. Drain on a paper towel until cool enough to crumble.
8. If cheese is melty and gooey after an hour, you're good to go. If not, cook for up to another hour on high.
9. When time is up, give the dip a good stir, and add cooked and crumbled bacon!

NUTRIENTS PER SERVING

Calories: 293 Fat: 9g Carbs: 9g Protein: 12g

SPINACH-ARTICHOKE DIP

PREPARATION TIME
5'

COOK TIME
4 H

SERVING
5

INGREDIENTS

- One 14-oz. can of drained artichoke hearts
- 10 oz. chopped fresh spinach
- ½ cup + 2 tbsp. full-fat plain Greek yogurt
- ½ cup shredded mozzarella cheese
- ½ cup grated parmesan cheese
- 6 tbsp. full-fat sour cream
- 2 tbsp. mayo
- 1 tsp. onion powder
- 1 tsp. garlic powder
- Salt and pepper to taste

DIRECTIONS

1. Chop artichoke into small pieces.
2. Add everything, including artichokes, to the slow cooker and stir.
3. Cook on high for 4 hours.
4. When time is up, the dip should be cheesy and gooey.

NUTRIENTS PER SERVING

Calories: 196 Fat: 13g Carbs: 9g Protein: 9g

CHAPTER 14.
SOUPS, STEWS AND CHILI

BEEF BARLEY SOUP

PREPARATION TIME
20'

COOK TIME
14 H

SERVING
8

INGREDIENTS

- 16 oz. round beef steak
- 2 tbsp. butter
- ¼ cup onions
- 3 cups water
- ½ cup barley
- ½ tsp. black pepper
- 2 cups beef broth
- 1 cup celery, diced
- ¼ tbsp. dried basil
- ¼ tsp. savory, ground
- 1 cup carrots, chopped
- ¾ oz. red wine

DIRECTIONS

1. Put water, beef steaks, barley, and beef broth in the one pot slow cooker and cover the lid.
2. Cook on Low for about 13 hours and add the remaining ingredients.
3. Cover and cook on Low for 1 more hour.
4. Dish out to serve hot.

NUTRIENTS PER SERVING

Calories: 211 Fat: 4g Carbs: 14g Protein: 12g

EASY CHICKEN SOUP

PREPARATION TIME
10'

COOK TIME
4 H

SERVING
4

INGREDIENTS

- 64 oz. chicken stock
- 1 yellow onion, chopped
- 2 celery stalks, chopped
- 2 tbsp. parsley, chopped
- 2 zucchinis, chopped
- ½ tsp. thyme, dried
- 3 carrots, chopped
- 2 tbsp. olive oil
- 2 chicken breasts, skinless and boneless
- A pinch of salt and black pepper

DIRECTIONS

1. Drizzle the oil in your slow cooker, add chicken breasts, carrots, onion, celery, zucchini, thyme, salt, pepper, and stock, toss, cover, and cook on High for 4 hours.
2. Shred the meat, divide it and the soup into bowls and serve with parsley sprinkled on top

NUTRIENTS PER SERVING

Calories: 211 Fat: 4g Carbs: 14g Protein: 12g

CHICKEN, CORN AND BEAN STEW

PREPARATION TIME
5'

COOK TIME
5 H

SERVING
10

INGREDIENTS

- 3 lb. chicken tenders
- 1 cup Parmesan cheese, shredded
- 1 can seasoned diced tomatoes
- 1 can chili beans
- 1 can corn, drained

DIRECTIONS

1. Arrange chicken at the bottom of a slow cooker and stir in the remaining ingredients.
2. Cover and cook on High for about 5 hours.
3. Sprinkle with Parmesan cheese and dish out to serve.

NUTRIENTS PER SERVING

Calories: 338 Fat: 14g Carbs: 5.9g Protein: 20g

HEARTY TURKEY CHILI

PREPARATION TIME
5'

COOK TIME
8 H

SERVING
5

INGREDIENTS

- 1lb. ground turkey breast
- ¼ cup olive oil
- ½ tsp. salt
- 1 can white beans, drained and rinsed
- 2 tsp. dried marjoram
- 1 large onion, chopped
- 1 green pepper, chopped
- 1 can diced tomatoes
- 2 tbsp. chili powder
- 4 garlic cloves, minced
- 1 can no-salt-added tomatoes

DIRECTIONS

1. Put olive oil, green peppers, onions, and garlic in the slow cooker and sauté for about 3 minutes.
2. Add the rest of the ingredients and cover the lid.
3. Cook on Low for about 8 hours and dish out in a bowl to serve hot.

NUTRIENTS PER SERVING

Calories: 350 Fat: 17.6g Carbs: 18g Protein: 30g

HAMBURGER SOUP

PREPARATION TIME	COOK TIME	SERVING
15'	7 H	8

INGREDIENTS

- 1lb. ground meat, cooked
- 1 can diced tomatoes
- 1 can lima beans
- Salt, to taste
- 2 tbsp. olive oil
- 1 can kidney beans
- 1 can mixed vegetables
- 1½ tsp. red chili powder
- 1 can beef broth

DIRECTIONS

1. Put olive oil and ground meat in a slow cooker and cook for about 5 minutes.
2. Transfer the remaining ingredients into the slow cooker and cover the lid.
3. Cook on Low for about 7 hours and ladle out into the serving bowl to serve hot.

NUTRIENTS PER SERVING

Calories: 262 Fat: 14.4g Carbs: 12.2g Protein 20g

SOUTHWESTERN TURKEY STEW

PREPARATION TIME	COOK TIME	SERVING
5'	7 H	6

INGREDIENTS

- 15 oz. ground turkey
- ½ cup red kidney beans
- ½ cup corn
- 2 cups diced canned tomatoes
- 1 cup red bell peppers, sliced
- ½ medium onion, diced
- ½ cup sour cream
- ½ cup cheddar cheese, shredded
- 1 garlic clove, minced
- 1½ medium red potatoes, cubed

DIRECTIONS

1. Put all the ingredients in a bowl except sour cream and cheddar cheese.
2. Transfer into the slow cooker and cook on Low for about 7 hours.
3. Stir in the sour cream and cheddar cheese.
4. Dish out in a bowl and serve hot.

NUTRIENTS PER SERVING

Calories: 332 Fat: 15.5g Carbs: 17.1g Protein: 27.7g

RABBIT STEW

PREPARATION TIME
5'

COOK TIME
4 H

SERVING
4

INGREDIENTS

- 1 lb. rabbit, cubed
- ½ cup celery, diced
- 1 sausage, cubed
- 1 bay leaf
- 1 garlic clove, diced
- 1 cup Swiss chards, stalks
- ½ can water chestnuts, diced
- 1 piece of bacon
- ½ cup apple cider vinegar
- 3 cups chicken broth
- ½ cup olive oil
- Salt and black pepper, to taste

DIRECTIONS

1. Marinate rabbit in olive oil and apple cider vinegar and keep aside overnight.
2. Put chicken broth in the slow cooker and warm it up.
3. Meanwhile, sear bacon and sausage in a pan and transfer it to the slow cooker.
4. Stir in the rest of the ingredients and cover the lid.
5. Cook on Low for about 8 hours and dish out to serve hot.

NUTRIENTS PER SERVING

Calories: 418 Fat: 30.7g Carbs: 2.7g Protein: 59g

CHEESY MEATBALL SOUP

PREPARATION TIME
5'

COOK TIME
8 H

SERVING
6

INGREDIENTS

- 1 lb. ground beef
- ½ green bell pepper, finely chopped
- ½ cup purple onion, chopped
- 2 cups organic beef broth
- ½ red bell pepper, finely chopped
- 1 celery stalk, chopped
- 5 large mushrooms, chopped
- 5 strips bacon
- 1 egg

- ¼ cup ground flax seed meal
- 1 tsp. oregano
- 1 tbsp. parsley
- ½ tsp. pepper
- 1 tsp. salt
- ½ tsp. garlic powder
- 4 tbsp. heavy white cream
- 8 slices American cheese
- 4 tbsp. water
- 4 tbsp. butter

DIRECTIONS

For meatballs:
1. Mix together the ingredients and roll into medium sized meatballs.
2. Put this mixture in the slow cooker along with the ingredients for stock and thoroughly stir.
3. Cover and cook on Low for about 8 hours.

For the cheese sauce:
4. Put all the ingredients in a microwave safe dish and microwave for about 3 minutes.
5. Add this cheese sauce to the soup, gently stirring.
6. Dish out and serve hot.

NUTRIENTS PER SERVING

Calories: 419 Fat: 32g Carbs: 3.7g Protein: 10g

MEXICAN CHICKEN STEW

PREPARATION TIME
5'

COOK TIME
9 H

SERVING
6

INGREDIENTS

- 3 chicken breasts, boneless and skinless
- 1 can black beans, not drained
- 1 can corn
- 2 cans diced tomatoes and chilies
- ½ cup sour cream
- 1 cup onions, optional
- ½ cup Mexican cheese, shredded

DIRECTIONS

1. Place chicken breasts at the bottom of the crock pot and top with tomatoes, beans, and corns.
2. Cover and cook on Low for about 9 hours.
3. Dish out and serve hot.

NUTRIENTS PER SERVING

Calories: 286 Fat: 12.7g Carbs: 16.8g Protein: 20g

CHILI RABBIT STEW

PREPARATION TIME
15'

COOK TIME
5 H

SERVING
6

INGREDIENTS

- 10 oz. rabbit, chopped
- 2 eggplants, chopped
- 1 zucchini, chopped
- 1 onion, chopped
- 2 cups water
- 1 tbsp. butter
- 1 tsp. salt
- 1 tsp. chili flakes

DIRECTIONS

1. Place the chopped eggplants, zucchini, onion, and rabbit in the slow cooker.
2. Add water, butter, salt, and chili flakes.
3. Stir the stew.
4. Cook the stew for 5 hours on Low.

NUTRIENTS PER SERVING

Calories: 168 Fat: 6g Carbs: 13.6g Protein: 16g

BEEF CHILI

PREPARATION TIME
5'

COOK TIME
3 H

SERVING
8

INGREDIENTS

- 2 lb. lean ground beef
- 29 oz. canned diced tomatoes, not drained
- 3 tbsp. chili powder
- 1 yellow onion, chopped
- ¼ cup tomato paste
- ½ cup saltine cracker crumbs, finely ground
- 1 jalapeno, minced
- 3 garlic cloves, minced
- 2 (16-ounce) cans red kidney beans, rinsed and drained
- 1 tsp. Kosher salt
- 1 tsp. ground cumin
- 1 tsp. black pepper

DIRECTIONS

1. Cook onions and beef over medium high heat in a pot until brown.
2. Transfer to the slow cooker along with the rest of the ingredients.
3. Cover and cook on high for about 3 hours and dish out to serve.

NUTRIENTS PER SERVING

Calories: 638 Fat: 9g Carbs: 78.9g Protein: 30g

BROCCOLI CHEESE SOUP

PREPARATION TIME
5'

COOK TIME
6 H

SERVING
6

INGREDIENTS

- 1½ cups heavy cream
- 2½ cups water
- ½ cup red bell pepper, chopped
- 2 cups broccoli, chopped, thawed, and drained
- 2 tbsp. chives, chopped
- ¾ tsp. salt
- 2 tbsp. butter
- ½ tsp. dry mustard
- 8 oz. cheddar cheese, shredded
- 4 cups chicken broth
- ¼ tsp. cayenne pepper

DIRECTIONS

1. Put all the ingredients in a slow cooker except chives and cheese and mix well.
2. Cover and cook on Low for about 6 hours.
3. Sprinkle with cheese and cook on Low for about 30 minutes.
4. Garnish with chives and serve hot.

NUTRIENTS PER SERVING

Calories: 353 Fat: 10g Carbs: 4g Protein: 30g

CREAM OF SWEET POTATO SOUP

PREPARATION TIME
5'

COOK TIME
6 H

SERVING
4

INGREDIENTS

- 24 oz. sweet potatoes, peeled and chopped
- 1 red onion, peeled and chopped
- 2 celery stalks, chopped
- 5 cups chicken stock
- 1 cup full-fat coconut milk, unsweetened

DIRECTIONS

1. Grease a 4-quart slow-cooker and add all the ingredients to it, apart from the coconut milk.
2. Season with salt and ground black pepper, and stir to combine.
3. Cover and seal the slow-cooker with its lid, and adjust the cook timer for 6 hours.
4. Allow to cook at a low heat setting.
5. Puree the soup using a stick blender until smooth, then stir in the coconut milk.
6. Continue cooking for 30 minutes and then ladle soup into warm bowls to serve.

NUTRIENTS PER SERVING

Calories: 163 Fat: 8.5g Carbs: 11.5g Protein: 4.6g

TACO SOUP

PREPARATION TIME
5'

COOK TIME
4 H

SERVING
8

INGREDIENTS

- 1lb. ground sausage
- 2 cans chopped tomatoes
- 2 tbsp. taco seasonings
- ½ lb. cream cheese
- 4 cups chicken broth

DIRECTIONS

1. Place a large skillet over medium heat, pour in a tbsp. of olive oil, then add the ground sausage.
2. Allow to cook for 7 to 10 minutes, until the meat is nicely browned.
3. In the meantime, place the remaining ingredients into the slow-cooker and stir until well mixed.
4. Drain the grease from the meat and add to the slow-cooker.
5. Stir all ingredients together until well-mixed, then cover and seal the slow-cooker with its lid.
6. Adjust the cook timer for 4 hours, and allow to cook at a low heat setting.
7. Garnish with cilantro and cheese and serve.

NUTRIENTS PER SERVING

Calories: 547 Fat: 20g Carbs: 5g Protein: 33g

CREAMY CAULIFLOWER SOUP

PREPARATION TIME
5'

COOK TIME
6 H

SERVING
6

INGREDIENTS

- 1 cauliflower head, cut into florets
- 1 tsp. minced garlic
- 4 oz. grated cheddar cheese
- 8 oz. heavy cream
- 4 cups chicken stock

DIRECTIONS

1. Grease a 4-quart slow-cooker and add the cauliflower florets, garlic, and stock.
2. Season with salt and ground black pepper, and stir until mixed.
3. Cover and seal slow-cooker with its lid, and adjust the cook timer for 4 to 6 hours, allowing to cook at a low heat setting.
4. Stir in the cream and the cheese, and blend until smooth using a stick blender.
5. Serve immediately.

NUTRIENTS PER SERVING

Calories: 290 Fat: 25g Carbs: 6g Protein: 10g

CREAMY CAULIFLOWER SOUP

PREPARATION TIME
5'

COOK TIME
5 H

SERVING
6

INGREDIENTS

- 4 chicken breasts, skinless
- 4 cups spaghetti squash
- 1/4 cup parsley, chopped
- 1/3 cup lemon juice, fresh
- 3 eggs
- 10 cups chicken stock

DIRECTIONS

1. Season the chicken with salt and ground black pepper, and add to a 4-quart slow-cooker.
2. Add the spaghetti squash, parsley, and chicken stock, and stir until well-mixed.
3. Cover and seal the slow-cooker with its lid, and adjust the cook timer for 4 to 5 hours, allowing to cook at a low heat setting.
4. Remove the chicken from the soup and shred using forks.
5. Return the shredded chicken to the slow-cooker.
6. Beat the egg and the lemon juice together in a bowl, then add one cup of the hot broth mixture, stirring continuously.
7. Add this heated lemon mixture to the slow-cooker, and stir until combined.
8. Adjust the seasoning, and ladle the soup into warmed bowls to serve.

NUTRIENTS PER SERVING

Calories: 289 Fats: 15g Carbs: 9g Protein: 33g

TUSCAN SOUP

PREPARATION TIME	COOK TIME	SERVING
5'	8 H	6

INGREDIENTS

- 6 oz. ground Italian sausage
- 8 oz. cauliflower florets
- 3 cups chopped kale
- 2 oz. chicken stock
- ½ cup heavy cream

DIRECTIONS

1. Place a large skillet over medium heat, pour a tbsp. of olive oil onto the pan, and add the ground sausage.
2. Cook for 7 to 10 minutes, until nicely browned.
3. Drain off the fat, and transfer the meat to the slow-cooker.
4. Add the cauliflower florets, kale, and chicken stock, and season with salt, ground black pepper, and red pepper flakes.
5. Stir until mixed, then cover and seal slow-cooker with its lid.
6. Adjust the cook timer for 8 hours and allow to cook at a low heat setting.
7. Gently stir in the cream, and serve immediately.

NUTRIENTS PER SERVING

Calories: 246 Fat: 19g Carbs: 3.3g Protein: 15g

CHAPTER 15.
CONDIMENTS, SAUCES & BROTHS

CHILI CONEY DOG SAUCE

PREPARATION TIME	COOK TIME	SERVING
20'	4 H	4

INGREDIENTS

- ½ lb. ground beef, extra lean
- 8oz. tomato sauce
- ¼ cup water
- ¼ tbsp. Worcestershire sauce
- ¼ cup onion, minced
- 1 tbsp. mustard, ground
- ½ tbsp. garlic powder
- ¼ tbsp. black pepper, freshly ground
- ¼ tbsp. chili powder
- 1/8 tbsp. cayenne pepper

DIRECTIONS

1. Cook beef in skillet until it's no longer pink. Break the beef into crumbles, then drain it.
2. Add the cooked beef to the slow cooker with the rest of the ingredients.
3. Cover the slow cooker and cook on low for 4 hours.
4. Serve the sauce as a hot dog topping. Enjoy.

NUTRIENTS PER SERVING

Calories: 118 Fat: 4g Carbs: 4g Protein: 12g

CUCUMBERS PORK BROTH

PREPARATION TIME	COOK TIME	SERVING
5'	6 H	4

INGREDIENTS

- 1 pork butt roast, bone-in
- 1 onion, peeled and quartered
- 12 baby cucumbers
- 2 celery stalks, halved
- 4 ½ cups water

DIRECTIONS

1. Add all ingredients to the slow cooker.
2. Cover the slow cooker and cook on low for 6 hours.
3. When the time has elapsed, strain and discard onions and celery, preserve pork and cucumbers.
4. Let rest to cool, then cover and refrigerate overnight.

NUTRIENTS PER SERVING

Calories: 119 Fat: 4g Carbs: 0g Protein: 22g

CHICKEN FEET BONE BROTH

PREPARATION TIME
5'

COOK TIME
12 H

SERVING
8

INGREDIENTS

- 12 chicken feet, pastured
- 16 cups water, filtered
- 1 tbsp. salt
- 1 sprig rosemary
- ½ inch fresh ginger

DIRECTIONS

1. Add chicken feet, with the outer membrane removed, to the slow cooker.
2. Add water until the feet are submerged. Cover the slow cooker and bring it to a boil.
3. Use a spoon to skim off any fat on top. Add salt, rosemary, and ginger, then cook on low for 12 hours.

NUTRIENTS PER SERVING

Calories: 103 Fat: 6g Carbs: 1.8g Protein: 10.6g

GINGERY HIGH COLLAGEN BONE BROTH

PREPARATION TIME	COOK TIME	SERVING
30'	10 H	8

INGREDIENTS

- 2 lb. chicken wings, cut into pieces
- 1 lb. chicken feet
- 1 onion
- 1 cucumber
- 1 stalk celery
- 8 garlic cloves, minced
- 1-inch ginger, minced
- 1 tbsp. salt
- ½ tbsp. black pepper
- 4 cups water

DIRECTIONS

1. Add all ingredients to the slow cooker. The water should submerge all the ingredients.
2. Cover and cook on high for 10 hours.

NUTRIENTS PER SERVING

Calories: 262 Fat: 4g Carbs: 3g Protein: 22g

NACHO CHEESE SAUCE

PREPARATION TIME
5'

COOK TIME
11 H

SERVING
16

INGREDIENTS

- 16 oz. cheddar cheese, extra sharp
- 2 tbsp. chia seeds
- 2 cans full-fat milk
- 1 tbsp. Franks Red hot sauce

DIRECTIONS

1. Add all the ingredients to the slow cooker.
2. Cover the slow cooker and cook on low for 1 to 2 hours
3. When the time has elapsed, give a good stir.
4. Serve and enjoy when warm. Add all the ingredients to the slow cooker.
5. Cover the slow cooker and cook on low for 1 to 2 hours.

NUTRIENTS PER SERVING

Calories: 172 Fat 7g Carbs: 5.5g Protein: 10g

CREAMY KETO CHEESE SAUCE

PREPARATION TIME
5'

COOK TIME
1 H

SERVING
8

INGREDIENTS

- 1 cup heavy cream
- 4 oz. sharp cheddar cheese, grated
- 2 tbsp. Dijon mustard

DIRECTIONS

1. Add all the ingredients to the slow cooker.
2. Cover the slow cooker and cook on low for 1 to 2 hours.

NUTRIENTS PER SERVING

Calories: 155 Fat: 11g Carbs: 1g Protein: 4g

TARRAGON MUSHROOM SAUCE

PREPARATION TIME
10'

COOK TIME
2 H

SERVING
4

INGREDIENTS

- 1 tbsp. butter
- 1 garlic clove, crushed
- 1 onion, thinly sliced
- ½ tbsp. salt
- Pinch pepper, ground
- 7 oz. mushrooms, thinly sliced
- 5 tbsp. Worcestershire sauce
- 1 tbsp. Dijon mustard
- ½ cup heavy cream
- 2 tbsp. tarragon, fresh and finely chopped

DIRECTIONS

1. Heat a skillet over high heat and sauté butter, garlic clove, onions, salt, and ground pepper until the onions are translucent.
2. Add mushrooms and cook for 3 minutes. Transfer to a slow cooker.
3. Add all other ingredients except tarragon, cover the slow cooker, and cook on low for 2 hours.
4. Stir in tarragon and serve. Enjoy.

NUTRIENTS PER SERVING

Calories: 166 Fat: 8g Carbs: 4g Protein: 3g

BUFFALO WING SAUCE

PREPARATION TIME
5'

COOK TIME
1 H

SERVING
6

INGREDIENTS

- ⅔ cup hot sauce (or Franks Red Hot pepper sauce)
- ½ cup butter, unsalted
- 1 ½ tbsp. white vinegar
- ¼ tbsp. Worcestershire sauce

DIRECTIONS

1. Add all ingredients in a slow cooker.
2. Give a good stir, cover, and cook on low for 1 hour or until bubbling.

NUTRIENTS PER SERVING

Calories: 151 Fat: 9g Carbs: 0.8g Protein: 4g

ALFREDO SAUCE

PREPARATION TIME
15'

COOK TIME
5 H

SERVING
12

INGREDIENTS

- Coconut oil spray
- 3 ½ cups chicken broth
- 2 cups heavy whipping cream
- 5 minced garlic cloves
- ½ cup soft butter
- ½ cup coconut flour
- ¼ cup fresh parsley, chopped
- 1 cup parmesan cheese, grated

DIRECTIONS

1. Spray the slow cooker with coconut oil spray.
2. Add chicken broth, whipping cream, and garlic.
3. Cover and cook for 5 hours.
4. Mix butter, flour, and parsley until well combined.
5. Stir in butter mixture into the slow cooker and cook for another 30 minutes.
6. Stir in parmesan cheese into slow cooker until well mixed.

NUTRIENTS PER SERVING

Calories: 273 Fat: 19 g Carbs: 7g Protein: 5g

CHICKEN AND CREAMY CHIVE SAUCE

PREPARATION TIME
15'

COOK TIME
5 H

SERVING
6

INGREDIENTS

- ¼ cup butter
- 10 ½ oz. Italian salad dressing mix
- 110 ¾ oz. golden mushroom soup, canned
- ½ cup dry white wine
- Half 8-oz. cream cheese spread tub with chives and onion
- 1 ½ lb. chicken breast halves, boneless and skinless

DIRECTIONS

1. Use a saucepan to melt the butter.
2. Stir in the Italian salad dressing, mushroom soup, wine, and cream cheese to the saucepan until well combined.
3. Place the chicken in the slow cooker and pour the sauce in the saucepan over the chicken.
4. Cover and cook for 5 hours.

NUTRIENTS PER SERVING

Calories: 253 Fat: 11g Carbs: 6g Protein: 28g

VEGETABLES AND CHEESE SAUCE

PREPARATION TIME
5'

COOK TIME
3 H

SERVING
6

INGREDIENTS

- 16 oz. thawed Italian vegetables, frozen
- 3 cups thawed broccoli florets, frozen
- 8 oz. cream cheese, sliced
- 1 ½ cups thawed kale, frozen, cut, and squeezed dry
- ⅓ cup chicken broth
- 1 tbsp. butter
- ¼ tbsp. salt
- ¼ tbsp. pepper

DIRECTIONS

1. Place the Italian vegetables, broccoli, cheese, kale, chicken broth, butter, salt, and pepper in a slow cooker.
2. Cover and cook for 3 hours and when all the cheese will have melted.
3. Remove the lid and stir the sauce.
4. Serve and enjoy.

NUTRIENTS PER SERVING

Calories: 240 Fat: 17g, Carbs: 14g Protein: 10g

BEER BLUE CHEESE SAUCE

PREPARATION TIME	COOK TIME	SERVING
5'	1 H	8

INGREDIENTS

- 8 oz. blue cheese
- 16 oz. cream cheese
- 1 cup yellow cheddar cheese, shredded
- 3 scallions, sliced and steam removed
- 1 tbsp. cayenne pepper, ground
- 12 oz. can Coors light

DIRECTIONS

1. In a slow cooker mix, the blue cheese, cream cheese, cheddar cheese, scallions, and cayenne pepper.
2. Pour the Coors light on top of the ingredients in the slow cooker.
3. Cover and cook for 1 hour, ensuring that you stir after every 20 minutes and all cheese will have melted.

NUTRIENTS PER SERVING

Calories: 356 Carbs: 4g Protein: 13g

PIZZA FONDUE SAUCE

PREPARATION TIME
5'

COOK TIME
3 H

SERVING
/

INGREDIENTS

- 1 lb. ground beef, lean
- 32 oz. pizza sauce
- 8 oz. mozzarella shredded cheese
- 8 oz. cheddar cheese, shredded
- 1 tbsp. oregano
- 2 tbsp. grated parmesan cheese
- Additional toppings of choice

DIRECTIONS

1. In a skillet, brown the beef, then drain excess fat.
2. Combine pizza sauce, beef, toppings of choice, and all other remaining ingredients in your slow cooker.
3. Cook while covered for 2-3 hours on low.
4. If desired, top with dollops of ricotta cheese in the last 30 minutes of cooking; just a few drops.

NUTRIENTS PER SERVING

Calories: 328 Fat: 39g Carbs: 12g Protein: 25.3g

CREAM GORGONZOLA SAUCE

PREPARATION TIME
5'

COOK TIME
1 H

SERVING
8

INGREDIENTS

- 2 cups heavy whipping cream
- 2tbsp. parmesan cheese, grated
- 4 oz. crumbled gorgonzola cheese
- ½ tbsp. Himalayan sea salt
- ½ tbsp. ground black pepper.

DIRECTIONS

1. In a slow cooker, heat the heavy cream until boiling.
2. Turn to low and let continue boiling to the desired thickness, about 40-50 minutes but don't over boil.
3. Turn off the heat, then add in all other ingredients and stir to combine.

NUTRIENTS PER SERVING

Calories: 236 Fat: 22g Carbs: 3g Protein: 4g

VODKA SAUCE

PREPARATION TIME
15'

COOK TIME
6 H

SERVING
5

INGREDIENTS

- Coconut oil spray
- 2 minced garlic cloves
- 1/2 chopped onion
- 1 tbsp. red pepper, crushed
- 15 oz. tomato sauce
- 1 tbsp. olive oil
- 1 cup beef broth
- 14 ½ oz. tomatoes, diced
- 5 chopped basil leaves
- 1 cup plain vodka
- ½ cup half & half
- Salt and pepper to taste

DIRECTIONS

1. Spray the slow cooker with coconut oil spray.
2. Add garlic, onion, red pepper, tomato sauce, olive oil, beef broth, tomatoes, basil, and plain vodka to the slow cooker and mix until well combined.
3. Cover the slow cooker and cook for 6 hours.
4. Whisk in half & half to the slow cooker and cook for another 15 minutes.

NUTRIENTS PER SERVING

Calories: 316 Fat: 11g Carbs: 13.9g Protein: 3.8g

CHAPTER 16.
VEGETABLES

SQUASH AND ZUCCHINI CASSEROLE

PREPARATION TIME
10'

COOK TIME
6 H

SERVING
6

INGREDIENTS

- 2 cups yellow squash, quartered and sliced
- 2 cups zucchini, quartered and sliced
- 1/4 cup Parmesan cheese, grated
- 1/4 cup butter, cut into pieces
- 1 tsp. garlic powder
- 1 tsp. Italian seasoning
- 1/4 tsp. pepper
- 1/2 tsp. sea salt

DIRECTIONS

1. Add sliced yellow squash and zucchini to a slow cooker.
2. Sprinkle with garlic powder, Italian seasoning, pepper, and salt.
3. Top with grated cheese and butter.
4. Cover with the lid and cook on low for 6 hours.

NUTRIENTS PER SERVING

Calories: 107 Fat: 9.5g Carbs: 2.5g Protein: 2.6g

ITALIAN ZUCCHINI

PREPARATION TIME	COOK TIME	SERVING
10'	3 H	3

INGREDIENTS

- 2 zucchinis, cut in half lengthwise then cut into half moons
- 1/4 cup Parmesan cheese, grated
- 1/2 tsp. Italian seasoning
- 1 tbsp. olive oil
- 1 tbsp. butter
- 2 garlic cloves, minced
- 1 onion, sliced
- 2 tomatoes, diced
- 1/2 tsp. pepper
- 1/4 tsp. salt

DIRECTIONS

1. Spray a slow cooker inside with cooking spray.
2. Add all ingredients except Parmesan cheese to the slow cooker and stir well.
3. Cover and cook on low for 3 hours.

NUTRIENTS PER SERVING

Calories: 181 Fat: 12.2g Carbs: 12g Protein: 7g

ALMOND GREEN BEANS

PREPARATION TIME
10'

COOK TIME
3 H

SERVING
4

INGREDIENTS

- 1 lb. green beans, rinsed and trimmed
- 1/2 cup almonds, sliced and toasted
- 1 cup vegetable stock
- 1/4 cup butter, melted
- 6 oz. onion, sliced
- 1 tbsp. olive oil
- 1/4 tsp. pepper
- 1/2 tsp. salt

DIRECTIONS

1. Heat the olive oil in a pan over medium heat.
2. Add onion to the pan and sauté until softened.
3. Transfer sautéed onion to a slow cooker.
4. Add remaining ingredients except for almonds to the slow cooker and stir well.
5. Cover and cook on low for 3 hours.
6. Top with toasted almonds and serve.

NUTRIENTS PER SERVING

Calories: 253 Fat: 21.6g Carbs: 14.5g Protein: 5g

EASY RANCH MUSHROOMS

PREPARATION TIME	COOK TIME	SERVING
10'	3 H	6

INGREDIENTS

- 2 lb. mushrooms, rinsed, pat dry
- 2 packets ranch dressing mix
- 3/4 cup butter, melted
- 1/4 cup fresh parsley, chopped

DIRECTIONS

1. Add all ingredients except parsley to a slow cooker and stir well.
2. Cover and cook on low for 3 hours.
3. Garnish with parsley and serve.

NUTRIENTS PER SERVING

Calories: 237 Fat: 23.5g Carbs: 5.2g Protein: 5g

ITALIAN MUSHROOMS

PREPARATION TIME
10'

COOK TIME
4 H

SERVING
6

INGREDIENTS

- 1 lb. mushrooms, cleaned
- 1 onion, sliced
- 1 packet Italian dressing mix
- 1/2 cup butter, melted

DIRECTIONS

1. Add onion and mushrooms to a slow cooker and mix well.
2. Combine butter and Italian dressing mix and pour over the onion and mushrooms.
3. Cover and cook on low for 4 hours.
4. Serve and enjoy.

NUTRIENTS PER SERVING

Calories 162 Fat: 15.6g Carbs: 4.8g Protein: 2.8g

GARLIC CHEESE SPINACH

PREPARATION TIME	COOK TIME	SERVING
10'	1 H	4

INGREDIENTS

- 16 oz. baby spinach
- 2 garlic cloves, minced
- 1 cup cheddar cheese, shredded
- 3 oz. cream cheese

DIRECTIONS

1. Add all ingredients to a slow cooker and stir well.
2. Cover and cook on high for 1 hour.
3. Stir well and serve.

NUTRIENTS PER SERVING

Calories: 216 Fat: 17.2g Carbs: 5.6g Protein: 12g

SIMPLE DILL CARROTS

PREPARATION TIME
10'

COOK TIME
2 H

SERVING
6

INGREDIENTS

- 1 lb. carrots, peeled and cut into round pieces on the diagonal
- 1 tbsp. butter
- 1 tbsp. fresh dill, minced
- 3 tbsp. water

DIRECTIONS

1. Add all ingredients to a slow cooker and stir well.
2. Cover and cook on low for 2 hours.
3. Stir well and serve.

NUTRIENTS PER SERVING

Calories: 49 Fat: 1.9g Carbs: 7.7g Protein: 0.7g

ROSEMARY GREEN BEANS

PREPARATION TIME
10'

COOK TIME
1,30 H

SERVING
4

INGREDIENTS

- 1 lb. Green beans, washed and trimmed
- 2 tbsp. fresh lemon juice
- 1 tsp. fresh thyme, minced
- 2 tbsp. water
- 1 tbsp. fresh rosemary, minced

DIRECTIONS

1. Add all ingredients to a slow cooker and stir well.
2. Cover and cook on low for 1 1/2 hours.
3. Stir well and serve.

NUTRIENTS PER SERVING

Calories: 40 Fat: 0.4g Carbs: 8.9g Protein: 2.2g

VEGETABLE STEW

PREPARATION TIME
10'

COOK TIME
2 H

SERVING
12

INGREDIENTS

- 3 cups carrots, shredded
- 32 oz. vegetable stock
- 1 cup cilantro, chopped
- 2 jalapeños, chopped
- 5 garlic cloves, minced
- 2 cups water
- 1 tbsp. cumin
- 1 tbsp. chili powder
- 2 tbsp. tomato paste
- 4 tomatoes, diced
- 1 large onion, diced
- 2 zucchinis, chopped
- 1/2 head cabbage, chopped
- Pepper
- Salt

DIRECTIONS

1. Add all ingredients to a slow cooker and stir well.
2. Cover and cook on low for 2 hours.
3. Stir well and serve.

NUTRIENTS PER SERVING

Calories: 57 Fat 0.9g Carbs: 10g Protein: 3.5g

TASTY VEGETABLE FAJITAS

PREPARATION TIME
10'

COOK TIME
3,30 H

SERVING
4

INGREDIENTS

- 1 cup cherry tomatoes, halved
- 3 bell peppers, cut into strips
- 1 onion, sliced
- 1 tsp. paprika
- 1 tbsp. olive oil
- Pepper and salt

DIRECTIONS

1. Cover and cook on high for 1 1/2 hours.
2. Add cherry tomatoes and cook for 2 hours longer.
3. Stir well and serve.

NUTRIENTS PER SERVING

Calories: 79g Fat: 3.9g Carbs: 11.4g Protein: 1.7g

SIMPLE ROASTED BROCCOLI

PREPARATION TIME
10'

COOK TIME
2 H

SERVING
4

INGREDIENTS

- 2 lb. broccoli florets
- 1 bell pepper, chopped
- 2 tsp. olive oil
- Pepper and salt

DIRECTIONS

1. Add all ingredients to a slow cooker and stir well to mix.
2. Cover and cook on high for 2 hours.
3. Stir well and serve.

NUTRIENTS PER SERVING

Calories: 89 Fat: 3.2g Carbs: 13.3g Protein: 7g

TOMATOES, GARLIC AND OKRA

PREPARATION TIME
10'

COOK TIME
2 H

SERVING
4

INGREDIENTS

- 1 1/2 cups okra, diced
- 1 small onion, diced
- 2 large tomatoes, diced
- 1 tsp. hot sauce
- 2 garlic cloves, minced

DIRECTIONS

1. Add all ingredients and stir well.
2. Cover and cook on low for 2 hours.
3. Stir well and serve.

NUTRIENTS PER SERVING

Calories: 41 Fat: 0.3g Carbs: 8.5g Protein: 1.8g

CHAPTER 17.
DESSERTS

ALMOND PUMPKIN CUSTARD

PREPARATION TIME
10'

COOK TIME
2 H

SERVING
6

INGREDIENTS

- 4 large eggs
- 4 tbsp. coconut oil, melted
- 1 tsp. pumpkin pie spice
- 1/2 cup almond flour
- 1 tsp. vanilla
- 1 cup pumpkin purée
- 1/2 cup Erythritol
- Pinch of salt

DIRECTIONS

1. Spray cooking spray.
2. Add eggs to a large mixing bowl and blend until smooth using a hand mixer. Slowly beat in the sweetener.
3. Add vanilla and pumpkin purée to the egg mixture and blend well.
4. Add almond flour, pumpkin pie spice, salt, and coconut oil and blend until well combined.
5. Pour mixture.
6. Cook on low for 2 hours 30 minutes.

NUTRIENTS PER SERVING

Calories: 196 Fat: 17.2g Carbs: 5.8g Protein: 6.7g

LEMON BLUEBERRY CAKE

PREPARATION TIME
10'

COOK TIME
3 H

SERVING
12

INGREDIENTS

- 6 eggs, separated
- ½ cup fresh blueberries
- 2 cups heavy cream
- 1/2 cup Swerve
- 1/3 cup fresh lemon juice
- 1 tsp. lemon zest
- 1/2 cup coconut flour
- 1/2 tsp. salt

DIRECTIONS

1. Add egg whites to a large mixing bowl and beat until stiff peaks form. Set aside.
2. In another bowl, whisk egg yolks with heavy cream, Swerve, lemon juice, lemon zest, coconut flour, and salt.
3. Slowly fold the egg whites into the egg yolk mixture until well combined.
4. Spray with cooking spray.
5. Pour prepared.
6. Sprinkle blueberries on top of batter.
7. Cook on low for 3 hours.

NUTRIENTS PER SERVING

Calories: 108 Fat: 9.7g Carbs: 2.2g Protein: 3.4g

TASTY LEMON CAKE

PREPARATION TIME	COOK TIME	SERVING
10'	3 H	8

INGREDIENTS

- 2 eggs
- Zest of 1 lemon
- 1 tbsp. lemon juice
- 1/2 cup whipping cream
- 1/2 cup butter, melted
- 2 tsp. baking powder
- 6 tbsp. Swerve
- 1/2 cup coconut flour
- 1 1/2 cups almond flour

For topping:
- 2 tbsp. fresh lemon juice
- 2 tbsp. butter, melted
- 1/2 cup hot water
- 3 tbsp. Swerve

DIRECTIONS

1. In a mixing bowl, mix together almond flour, baking powder, Swerve, and coconut flour.
2. In a large bowl, whisk together eggs, lemon zest, 1 tbsp. lemon juice, butter, and whipping cream.
3. Add almond flour mixture to the egg mixture and stir until well combined.
4. Spray the inside of a slow cooker with cooking spray.
5. Pour batter into the slow cooker and spread well.
6. Combine together all topping ingredients and pour over the cake batter.
7. Cover and cook on high for 3 hours.

NUTRIENTS PER SERVING

Calories: 294 Fat: 28.5g Carbs: 7.4g Protein: 6.3g

ALMOND & CHOCO CAKE

PREPARATION TIME
15'

COOK TIME
3,30 H

SERVING
8

INGREDIENTS

- 1 cup + 2 tbsp. almond flour
- 1/3 cup cocoa powder (unsweetened)
- ½ cup sweetener
- 1 tsp. vanilla
- 1 ½ tbsp. baking powder
- 6 tbsp. butter, unsalted, melted
- 2 large eggs
- ½ cup almond milk

Optional:
- ½ low carb chocolate chips

DIRECTIONS

1. Spray a slow cooker with a cooking spray of your choice.
2. Mix flour, cocoa powder, sweetener, baking powder, and salt in a bowl.
3. Add eggs (beaten), butter, almond milk, vanilla extract (and optional: choco chips)
4. Place in the slow cooker and cook on a low setting for 3 hours.
5. Let stand for 30 minutes before serving.

NUTRIENTS PER SERVING

Calories: 216 Fat: 18.8g Carbs: 4g Protein: 8g

RICE PUDDING

PREPARATION TIME
5'

COOK TIME
3,30 H

SERVING
6

INGREDIENTS

- 7-oz. no carb rice (Shirataki rice)
- 2 large eggs
- ¼ cup sweetener
- 1 tsp. vanilla extract
- ½ unsweetened coconut, shredded
- 15-oz. can coconut cream
- ½ tsp. cinnamon

DIRECTIONS

1. Spray the inside of a slow cooker with your choice of cooking spray.
2. Wash rice well, then in a saucepan, heat it on low heat until well dried.
3. Mix eggs, sweetener, coconut cream, shredded coconut, and vanilla, and place them in the slow cooker.
4. Add rice and stir in until well mixed.
5. Cover and set heat to high and cook for 3 ½ hours.
6. Add cinnamon before serving.

NUTRIENTS PER SERVING

Calories: 338 Fat: 29g Carbs: 4.8g Protein: 7.2g

CHOCO BLACKBERRY CAKE

PREPARATION TIME
15'

COOK TIME
3 H

SERVING
6

INGREDIENTS

- 1 cup almond flour
- ½ cup coconut flakes, unsweetened
- ¼ coconut oil
- ¼ choco powder, unsweetened
- 2 large eggs
- ¼ tsp. sweetener
- 1 tsp. baking soda
- 1/8 cup ghee
- ¼ heavy cream
- 1/8 tsp. salt
- 1 cup blackberries
- ¼ low choco chips, unsweetened

DIRECTIONS

1. Spray slow cooker with a cooking spray of your choice or with ghee
2. Combine almond flour, sweetener, coconut, choco powder, baking soda, and salt
3. Add eggs, coconut oil, heavy cream, and ghee until well mixed.
4. Add blackberries and optionally choco chips.
5. Place in the slow cooker and set on low for 3 hours.
6. Let the cake get cooled.

Tasty suggestion:
7. Add one more cup of hot blackberries as topping.
8. Enjoy!

NUTRIENTS PER SERVING

Calories: 318 Fat: 20g Carbs: 9g Protein: 8.2g

APPLE CRISP

PREPARATION TIME
10'

COOK TIME
4 H

SERVING
6

INGREDIENTS

- 3 Granny Smith apples, cored and chopped
- 1 cup almond flour
- ½ tsp. ground cinnamon
- 1/8 cup sweetener (Erythritol or Swerve)
- ¼ tsp. ground nutmeg
- 1/8 salt
- ¼ coconut oil
- ½ vanilla extract
- 1/8 tsp. salt

DIRECTIONS

1. Spray slow cooker with a cooking spray.
2. Mix together the apples and cinnamon.
3. Place the apple mix in the slow cooker.
4. Mix the almond flour, sweetener, salt, nutmeg, vanilla, coconut oil, and butter together with a fork until crumbly.
5. Sprinkle the crumble mixture over the apples evenly.
6. Cook on a low setting for 4 to 6 hours.

NUTRIENTS PER SERVING

Calories: 225 Fat: 19g Carbs: 9g Protein: 4g

COCONUT PUMPKIN PIE

PREPARATION TIME
15'

COOK TIME
3 H

SERVING
16

INGREDIENTS

For the crust:
- ¾ cup coconut, shredded, unsweetened
- ¼ sweetener (Erythritol, Stevia, Swerve)
- 4 tbsp. butter, unsalted, melted
- ¼ cup cocoa powder, unsweetened
- 1/3 salt

For the filling:
- 1 cup heavy cream

- 4 large eggs
- 2 cup canned pumpkin (not pie mix)
- 1 tbsp. vanilla extract
- ½ tsp. pumpkin pie spice
- 1 tsp. cinnamon
- ½ tsp. salt

DIRECTIONS

1. Spray pan with a cooking spray of your choice. Mix the crust ingredients together in the food processor until crumbs.
2. Press the mixture into the pan on the bottom and an inch up the sides of the pan
3. Add the filling ingredients, except eggs and sugar, to an electronic mixer at medium speed.
4. Gradually add sugar, and beat in the eggs one by one.
5. Spoon ¾ of the mixture into the pan and spread evenly.
6. Beat the pumpkin spice into the remaining cream cheese mix and pour onto the crust.
7. Cook on low heat setting for 3 hours.
8. Uncover and let it cool ½ hour, then refrigerate for 3 hours.
9. Slice and enjoy!

NUTRIENTS PER SERVING 1 SLICE

Calories: 170 Fat: 15 g Carbs: 6g Protein: 4.2g

APPLE DESSERT

PREPARATION TIME
10'

COOK TIME
4 H

SERVING
10

INGREDIENTS

- Cooking spray
- 5/6 Granny Smith apples, peeled and sliced
- ¼ granulated sugar
- ½ cup oats
- 15 oz. yellow cake mix (1 box)
- ½ cupbutter, sliced
- 1 tsp. cinnamon

DIRECTIONS

1. Coat your slow cooker with oil.
2. Place apple in the slow cooker. Spread the sugar + ½ tsp. Cinnamon.
3. Mix well in a bowl the cake mix, oats, and ½ tsp. cinnamon. Pour onto the apples, and add the slices of the butter over the top of the cake mix.
4. Cook on high for 4 hours, checking each 1 hour.

Tasty suggestion:
5. Serve with ice cream.
6. Enjoy!

NUTRIENTS PER SERVING

Calories 85 Fat: 1g Carbs: 19g Protein: 1 g

CHAI APPLE BUTTER

PREPARATION TIME
5'

COOK TIME
7 H

SERVING
28

INGREDIENTS

- 5 lb. apples, peeled and sliced
- 1 tbsp. brown sugar
- 1/2 tsp. salt
- 2 tsp. ground turmeric
- 2 tsp. ground cardamom
- 2 tsp. ground coriander
- 2 tsp. ground cinnamon

DIRECTIONS

1. Put all the ingredients in a slow cooker.
2. Cook for 5 hours on high.
3. Uncover and stir occasionally.

NUTRIENTS PER SERVING

Calories: 53 Fat: 0g Carbs: 14g Protein: 0g

DELICIOUS CHOCO CAKE

PREPARATION TIME
10'

COOK TIME
3 H

SERVING
12

INGREDIENTS

- ½ cup almond flour
- 1 cup sweetener
- 4 tbsp. unsweetened cocoa power
- ½ cup butter, melted
- 4 eggs
- 2 egg yolks
- 1 tsp. baking soda
- 1 tsp. vanilla extract
- ½ tsp. salt
- 2 cups hot water
- 4 oz. cocoa chips (unsweetened)

DIRECTIONS

1. Coat your slow cooker with oil.
2. In a bowl, combine ½ cup swerve, flour, 2 tbsp. cocoa powder, baking soda, and salt.
3. In a second smaller bowl, mix the cooled melted butter with eggs, yolks, and vanilla extract.
4. Pour the wet ingredients in the bowl with the dry ingredients, stir until well mixed and place in the slow cooker.
5. Add the choco chips.
6. Mix the remaining cocoa powder and sweetener with hot water and add on the top of the choco chips.
7. Cook on low for 3 hours.
8. Let cool and serve.

NUTRIENTS PER SERVING

Calories: 157 Fat: 12g Carbs: 10g Protein: 3.8g

APPLE CONFIT

PREPARATION TIME
5'

COOK TIME
2 H

SERVING
8

INGREDIENTS

- 3 lb. firm cooking apples, sliced
- 1/2 tsp. ground cinnamon
- 1/4 cup sugar
- 1 tsp. vanilla extract

DIRECTIONS

1. Toss the apple slices in cinnamon and sugar.
2. Put the apple slices in the slow cooker.
3. Cook on high for 2 hours.
4. Stir in the vanilla.
5. Put in the refrigerator and chill for a few hours before serving.

NUTRIENTS PER SERVING

Calories: 108 Fat: 0g Protein: 0g Carbs: 28g

RASPBERRY CHOCO CAKE

PREPARATION TIME
10'

COOK TIME
3 H

SERVING
10

INGREDIENTS

- 1 cup almond flour
- ¼ cup cocoa powder, unsweetened
- ½ cup sweetener
- 3 eggs
- 2 oz. choco chips, unsweetened
- ¼ tsp. salt
- ½ butter, unsalted, cut into large pieces
- 1 tsp. vanilla extract
- ½ cup heavy cream
- 1 cup raspberries

DIRECTIONS

1. Coat your slow cooker with oil.
2. Combine the cocoa, flour, sweetener, baking soda, and salt.
3. Heat choco chips and butter until melt, let cool.
4. In a bowl, combine beat eggs until frothy, beat in the heavy cream, add vanilla extract and mix all together wet and dry ingredients.
5. Wait for chocolate cooled enough, put in the batter, and mix well.
6. Pour in raspberries.
7. Place in the slow cooker, set on low, and cook for 3 hours.
8. Let cool and serve.
9. Enjoy!

NUTRIENTS PER SERVING

Calories: 245 Fat: 27g Carbs: 6.8g Protein: 4.5g

CHAPTER 18.
SPECIAL SECTION 1: BREAD

ZUCCHINI BREAD

PREPARATION TIME
60'

COOK TIME
3 H

SERVING
10

INGREDIENTS

- 2 small zucchinis, grated, about 8 oz. by weight
- 1 cup almond flour
- ½ cup flaxseed meal
- ½ cup shredded coconut, unsweetened
- 4 tbsp. protein powder
- 2 tbsp. stevia powder
- 2 tsp. baking powder
- 1 tsp. kosher salt, divided
- 2 tsp. cinnamon powder
- ½ tsp. ground cardamom
- ¼ tsp. organic nutmeg powder
- ¼ freshly ground sweet-scented pepper
- ½ cup chopped nuts
- 3 eggs
- 4 tbsp. ghee, melted
- ½ tsp. liquid stevia extract (or on your taste)
- 3-4 tbsp. water

DIRECTIONS

1. Put grated zucchinis in a big strainer over a bowl. Do not put anything in the bowl. Take half of the salt and sprinkle over the zucchini. This technique will remove its moisture.
2. Meanwhile, in a mixing bowl, combine the dry ingredients: almond flour, flaxseed meal, shredded coconut, protein powder, stevia powder, baking powder, the rest of salt, cinnamon powder, ground cardamom, nutmeg powder, sweet-scented ground pepper, and chopped nuts.
3. In a separate bowl, mix in the rest of the ingredients: eggs, melted ghee, stevia extract, and water. Add squeezed zucchinis too.
4. Gradually add the dry flour-spices mixture into the wet mixture. Stir until well mixed.
5. Line your slow cooker with a parchment paper or grease the inner part of the pot all over. Pour in the batter. Let it cooked on high for at most 5 hours. Make sure to let it rest for slicing.
6. Smart suggestion: if you love crusty loaves, run the loaf under the broiler for a few minutes for firm up the crust.

NUTRIENTS PER SERVING

calories 175, fat 13.7g, carbs 6.1g, protein 8.9g

DELICIOUS BREAD PUDDING

PREPARATION TIME
10'

COOK TIME
4 H

SERVING
8

INGREDIENTS

- 5 eggs
- 8 cups of bread cubes
- 1 tbsp. vanilla
- 4 cups milk
- 3/4 cup maple syrup
- 1 tbsp. cinnamon

DIRECTIONS

1. In a large bowl, whisk together eggs, sugar, cinnamon, vanilla, and milk.
2. Line your slow cooker with a parchment paper or grease the inner part of the pot all over.
3. Add bread cubes into the cooking pot.
4. Pour egg mixture on top of bread cubes and let sit for 15 minutes.
5. Select slow cook mode and cook on High for 4 hours, checking first time after 1 hour and then every half an hour.
6. Smart suggestion: if you love crusty loaves, run the loaf under the broiler for a few minutes for firm up the crust.
7. Serve and enjoy.

NUTRIENTS PER SERVING

calories 153, fat 4.74g, carbs 23.26g, protein 5.27g

BASIL CHEESE BREAD

PREPARATION TIME
10'

COOK TIME
4 H

SERVING
10

INGREDIENTS

- 2 cups almond flour
- 1 cup warm water
- ½ tsp. salt
- 1 tsp. basil dried
- ½ cup mozzarella, shredded
- 1 tsp. active dry yeast
- 2 tsp. melted unsalted butter
- 2 tsp. sweetener

DIRECTIONS

1. In a mixing container, combine the almond flour, dried basil, salt, shredded mozzarella cheese, and stevia powder.
2. Get another container, where you will combine the warm water and the melted unsalted butter.
3. Gradually mix all ingredients, stir well.
4. Line your slow cooker with a parchment paper or grease the inner part of the pot all over.
5. Pour the mixture in the slow cooker, set on High and cook for 4 hours, checking first time after 1 hour and then every half an hour.
6. Smart suggestion: if you love crusty loaves, run the loaf under the broiler for a few minutes for firm up the crust.

NUTRIENTS PER SERVING

calories: 124, fat: 8g, carb: 3.8g, protein: 11g

AMERICAN CHEESE BEER BREAD

PREPARATION TIME
5'

COOK TIME
4 H

SERVING
10

INGREDIENTS

- ½ cups of fine almond flour
- ¾ tsp.unsalted melted butter
- 1 tsp. salt
- 1 egg
- 2 tsp. swerve sweetener
- 1 cup keto low-carb beer
- 1 tsp. baking powder
- 1 cup of cheddar cheese, shredded
- 1 tsp. active dry yeast

DIRECTIONS

1. Prepare a mixing container, where you will combine the almond flour, swerve sweetener, salt, shredded cheddar cheese, and baking powder.
2. Prepare another mixing container, where you will combine the unsalted melted butter, egg, and low- carb keto beer.
3. Gradually mix all ingredients, stir well.
4. Line your slow cooker with a parchment paper or grease the inner part of the pot all over.
5. Pour in the slow cooker, set on High and cook for 4 hours, checking first time after 1 hour and then every half an hour.
6. Smart suggestion: if you love crusty loaves, run the loaf under the broiler for a few minutes for firm up the crust.

NUTRIENTS PER SERVING

calories: 94, fat: 6g, carb: 4g, protein: 1g

PARMESAN CHEDDAR BREAD

PREPARATION TIME
5'

COOK TIME
4 H

SERVING
10

INGREDIENTS

- 1 cup parmesan cheese grated
- 1 cup almond flour
- 1 tsp. baking powder
- ¾ tsp. salt
- ¼ tsp. cayenne pepper
- ½ cup unsweetened almond milk
- 1/3 cup sour cream
- 1 tsp. active dry yeast
- 2 tsp. unsalted melted butter
- 1 egg

DIRECTIONS

1. Get a container for mixing, and combine the almond flour, shredded parmesan cheese, cayenne pepper, baking powder, and salt.
2. In another mixing container, combine the unsweetened almond milk, sour cream, egg, and unsalted melted butter.
3. Gradually mix all ingredients, stir well.
4. Line your slow cooker with a parchment paper or grease the inner part of the pot all over.
5. Pour in the slow cooker, set on High and cook for 4 hours, checking first time after 1 hour and then every half an hour.
6. Smart suggestion: if you love crusty loaves, run the loaf under the broiler for a few minutes for firm up the crust.
7.

NUTRIENTS PER SERVING

Calories: 134 Fat: 6.8g Carb: 4.2g Protein: 12g

PEPPER CHEDDAR BREAD

PREPARATION TIME
5'

COOK TIME
5 H

SERVING
10

INGREDIENTS

- ½ cup coconut flour
- 1 cup of almond blanched fine flour
- 1 tsp. black pepper powder
- ¾ cup of warm water
- 1 cup cheddar cheese, grated
- 1 tsp. salt
- 2 tsp. unsalted melted butter
- 1 tsp. baking powder
- 1 tsp. active dry yeast

DIRECTIONS

1. Get a container for mixing, and combine the almond flour, coconut flour, shredded cheddar cheese, black pepper powder, baking powder, and salt.
2. Get another container, where you will combine the warm water and unsalted melted butter.
3. Gradually mix all ingredients, stir well.
4. Line your slow cooker with a parchment paper or grease the inner part of the pot all over.
5. Pour in the slow cooker, set on High and cook for 4 hours, checking first time after 1 hour and then every half an hour.
6. Smart suggestion: if you love crusty loaves, run the loaf under the broiler for a few minutes for firm up the crust.

NUTRIENTS PER SERVING

Calories: 84 Fat: 4g Carb: 3g Protein: 1g

CHAPTER 19.
SPECIAL SECTION 2: EXTRA YUMMY MEALS

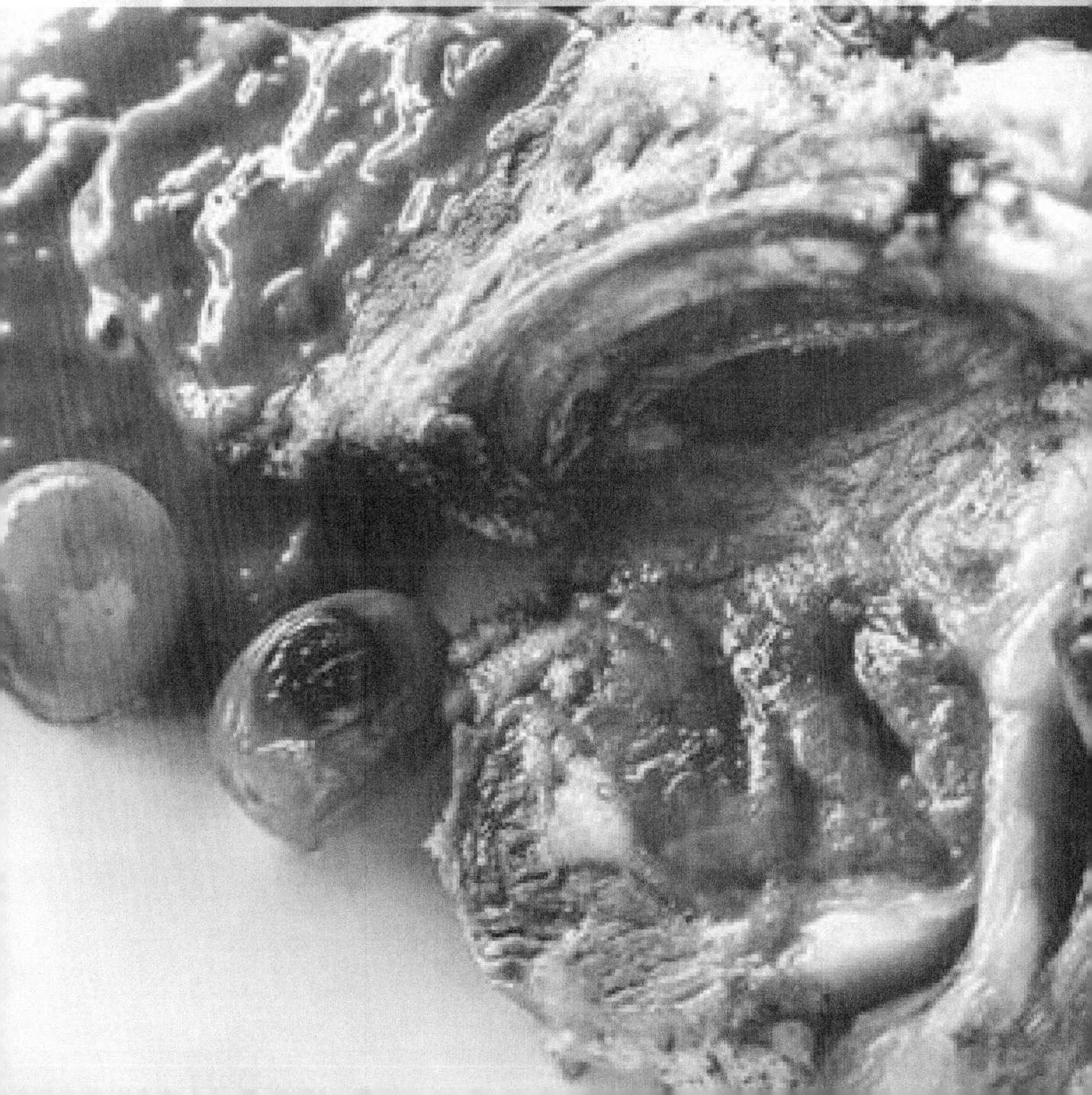

DELIGHTFUL SPICY BEEF

PREPARATION TIME
5'

COOK TIME
10 H

SERVING
4

INGREDIENTS

- 2 lb. of beef chuck on the bone
- 1 can chopped tomatoes
- 1 can chipotle sauce
- 1 can drained diced jalapeño chilies
- 1 chopped onion
- 3 cloves of minced garlic
- 2 tbsp. of chili powder
- 1 tbsp. honey
- 2 ½ tsp. kosher salt
- 1 tsp. ground cumin
- 2 cups beef broth

DIRECTIONS

1. Put all the ingredients into a slow cooker.
2. Cover and cook on low for 8 to 10 hours until the beef becomes tender.
3. Take the lid off the slow cooker during the last ½ hour to thicken the sauce.
4. Take the beef out and use a fork to shred it, and mix into the sauce in the slow cooker.
5. Divide onto plates and serve.

NUTRIENTS PER SERVING

Calories: 261 Fat:11g Carbs: 5.5g Protein: 30g

TASTY SPICED CHILI BEEF EYE ROAST

PREPARATION TIME
5'

COOK TIME
8 H

SERVING
4

INGREDIENTS

- 3 lb. lean ground beef eye roast
- 2 tbsp. Worcestershire sauce
- 4 tbsp. fresh lime juice
- 1 ½ cups diced onions
- 1 cup diced red bell pepper
- 3 cloves minced garlic
- 3 minced and seeded Serrano chilies
- Salt and pepper
- ½ cup beef broth
- 1 cup canned tomatoes, diced
- ½ tsp. dried oregano

DIRECTIONS

1. Use salt and pepper to season the beef and put it into the slow cooker.
2. In a large bowl, whisk the remaining ingredients together and pour them over the beef.
3. Cook on low for 8 hours.
4. Use 2 forks to shred the beef

NUTRIENTS PER SERVING

Calories: 247 Carbs: 5.8g Fat: 6g Protein: 40g

SPECTACULAR MEATY CRUSHED TOMATO BOLOGNESE

PREPARATION TIME
5'

COOK TIME
6 H

SERVING
4

INGREDIENTS

- 4 oz. chopped pancetta
- 1 tbsp. butter
- 1 white onion, minced
- 2 stalks celery, minced
- 2 carrots, minced
- 2 lb. ground beef, 95% lean
- ¼ cup white wine
- 2 cans crushed tomatoes
- 3 bay leaves
- Salt and pepper

- ¼ cup chopped fresh parsley
- ½ cup half and half

DIRECTIONS

1. In a deep pan on low heat, sauté the pancetta for 4-5 minutes.
2. Add the carrots, onions, celery, and butter and cook for another 5 minutes.
3. Turn the heat up to medium, add the meat and the pepper and sauté until the meat browns.
4. Drain the fat, add the wine and cook for a further 3-4 minutes.
5. Pour the mixture into the slow cooker, add salt and pepper, the tomatoes, and bay leaves.
6. Cover and cook on low for 6 hours.
7. Add the half and half and the parsley.
8. Pour over pasta and serve.

NUTRIENTS PER SERVING

Calories: 143 Fat: 7g Carbs: 5.4g Protein: 15g

WONDERFUL BEEF & BACON MEATBALLS

PREPARATION TIME
5'

COOK TIME
6 H

SERVING
4

INGREDIENTS

- 2lb. ground beef
- 2 slices diced bacon
- 1 quartered onion
- 2 cloves garlic
- 1 egg
- Salt and pepper
- A handful of herbs of your choice
- 14 oz. canned chopped tomatoes

DIRECTIONS

1. Combine the garlic, onion, and bacon in a food processor and work until finely chopped.
2. Add the remaining ingredients except the tomatoes and work until the ingredients turn into a smooth paste.
3. Use your hands to mold the ingredients into meatballs and arrange them in a greased slow cooker.
4. Pour the canned tomatoes over the top, cover, and cook on high for 4-6 hours.

NUTRIENTS PER SERVING

Calorie:s 358 Fat: 22g Carbs: 5.2g Protein: 32g

YUMMY CABBAGE ROLLS AND CORNED BEEF

PREPARATION TIME
5'

COOK TIME
6 H

SERVING
4

INGREDIENTS

- 2 lb. corned beef
- 1 sliced onion
- 1 lemon
- ¼ cup coffee
- ¼ cup white wine
- 1 tbsp. bacon fat
- 1 tbsp. brown mustard
- 1 tbsp. Erythritol
- 2 tsp. kosher salt
- 2 tsp. Worcestershire sauce

- 1 tsp. peppercorns
- ¼ tsp. allspice
- 1 crushed bay leaf
- 15 Savoy cabbage leaves

DIRECTIONS

1. Add the liquids, spices, and the beef to the slow cooker.
2. Cover and cook for 6 hours on low.
3. Boil a saucepan of water and add the onions and the cabbage; boil for approximately 2-3 minutes or until the cabbage leaves are soft.
4. Pour ice-cold water into a bowl and add the cabbage leaves; allow them to soak for 3-4 minutes.
5. Slice the meat and other ingredients onto the cabbage leaves and roll them tightly.
6. Squeeze the lemon over the top and serve.

NUTRIENTS PER SERVING

Calories: 478 Fat: 25g Carbs: 3.8g Protein: 34.2g

DELICIOUS ONE-POT ORIENTAL LAMB

PREPARATION TIME
5'

COOK TIME
4 H

SERVING
4

INGREDIENTS

- 3 cups boneless lamb, diced
- 2 tbsp. almond flour
- 2 cups fresh spinach
- 2 halved small red onions
- 2 cloves minced garlic
- ¼ cup diced yellow turnip
- 2 tbsp. dry sherry
- 2-3 bay leaves
- 1 tsp. hot mustard
- ¼ tsp. ground nutmeg

- 1 tsp. fresh chopped thyme
- 1 tsp. fresh chopped rosemary
- 5-6 whole pimentoes
- 1 1/3 cups your preferred broth
- Salt and pepper
- 8 halved baby zucchinis
- 2 tbsp. olive oil

DIRECTIONS

1. Arrange the lamb in the slow cooker, pour the almond flour over the top.
2. Add the rest of the ingredients, cover, and cook for 4 hours on high.
3. Serve with a salad of your choice.

NUTRIENTS PER SERVING

Calories: 510 Fat: 37g Carbs: 24g Protein: 50g

CHAPTER 20.
2-WEEK MEAL PLAN

Week 01

Day 1

- Breakfast: Zucchini Casserole
- Lunch: Butter Chicken
- Snack: Buffalo Meatballs
- Dinner: Poached Salmon with Lemon
- Dessert: Almond Pumpkin Custard

Total net carbs: 21.9g

Day 2

- Breakfast: Avocado and Zucchini Bake
- Lunch: Corned Beef
- Snack: Garlicky Bacon Slice
- Dinner: Seafood Stew
- Dessert: Lemon Blueberry Cake

Total net carbs: 20.4g

Day 3

- Breakfast: Keto Porridge
- Lunch: Lamb in Curry Sauce
- Snack: Sardine Paté
- Dinner: Tilapia in Lemon Pepper Sauce
- Dessert: Chai Apple Butter

Total net carbs: 37g

Day 4

- Breakfast: Beef Casserole
- Lunch: Salmon and Scalloped Potatoes
- Snack: Spinach Mussels Salad
- Dinner: Pulled Pork
- Dessert: Almond & Choco Cake

Total net carbs: 34.3g

Day 5

- Breakfast: Shrimp Casserole
- Lunch: Special Seafood Chowder
- Snack: Glazed Walnuts
- Dinner: Tuscan Chicken
- Dessert: Rice Pudding

Total net carbs: 29.6g

Day 6

- Breakfast: Breakfast Frittata
- Lunch: Hearty White Fish Stew
- Snack: Italian Zucchini
- Dinner: Pork Roast
- Dessert: Delicious Choco Cake

Total net carbs: 33g

Day 7

- Breakfast: Salmon Cutlets
- Lunch: Sweet Lamb Tangine
- Snack: Blue Cheese Parsley Dip
- Dinner: Garlic Cheese Spinach
- Dessert: Apple Dessert

Total net carbs: 41.74g

Week 02

Day 1

- Breakfast: Ham and Kale Bake
- Lunch: Coconut Basil Curry Chicken
- Snack: Broccoli Dip
- Dinner: Spare Ribs
- Dessert: Tasty Lemon Cake

Total net carbs: 38g

Day 2

- Breakfast: Lemon Pancake
- Lunch: Chili Shrimps
- Snack: Choco Roasted Almonds
- Dinner: Cabbage Roll Soup
- Dessert: Choco Blackbarry Cake

Total net carbs: 33.5g

Day 3

-
- Breakfast: Cinnamon Eggs
- Lunch: Almond Green Beans
- Snack: Cheese Crackers
- Dinner: Rosemary Leg of Lamb
- Dessert: Coconut Pumpkin Pie

Total net carbs: 29g

Day 4

- Breakfast: Dill and Avocado Frittata
- Lunch: Creamy Chicken Thighs
- Snack: Keto Chocolate Pudding
- Dinner: Taco Soup
- Dessert: Chai Apple Butter

Total net carbs: 39.3g

Day 5

- Breakfast: Keto Lasagna
- Lunch: Peppered Steak
- Snack: Honey Chicken Wings
- Dinner: Cheese-Stuffed Turkey Meatballs
- Dessert: Delicious Choco Cake

Total net carbs: 34.9g

Day 6

- Breakfast: Chili Bake
- Lunch: Rabbit Stew
- Snack: Goat Cheese Dumplings
- Dinner: Flavored Tilapia
- Dessert: Almond & Choco Cake

Total net carbs: 28.9g

Day 7

- Breakfast: Sausage and Spinach
- Lunch: Duck Breast
- Snack: Cashew Dip
- Dinner: Lamb Meatballs
- Dessert: Lemon Blueberry Cake

Total net carbs: 22.9g

APPENDIX:
MEASUREMENTS & CONVERSIONS

ABBREVIATIONS

Tablespoon--tbsp.
Teaspoon--tsp.
Pound--lb.
Ounce--oz.
Gallon--gal.

CONVERSIONS

¼ tsp. = 1 ml
½ tsp. = 2 ml
1 tsp. = 5 ml
1 tbsp. = 15 ml
¼ cup = 59 ml
½ cup = 118 ml
½ oz. = 15 g

1 cup = 235 ml
1 oz. = 30 g
2 oz. = 60 g
4 oz. = 115 g
8 oz. = 225 g
12 oz. = 340 g
16 oz. or 1 lb. = 455 g

Printed in Great Britain
by Amazon